The Marion Press certifies that only one hundred copies of "Letters of Hawthorne to William D. Ticknor have been printed, from type, on Holland handmade paper, and bound in two volumes. The work was begun in August, 1909, and completed in April, 1910.

This copy is number 2 4

LETTERS OF HAWTHORNE TO
WILLIAM D. TICKNOR

LETTERS OF
HAWTHORNE
TO WILLIAM D. TICKNOR

1851 – 1864

NEWARK NEW JERSEY

THE CARTERET BOOK CLUB

1910

Reprinted with a
Foreword by C. E. Frazer Clark, Jr.
by

 Microcard Editions

1972

Reprinted in 1972 by NCR/Microcard
Editions, 901 26th Street, N.W., Washington, D.C., 10037 From a copy owned
by C. E. Frazer Clark, Jr., Bloomfield
Hills, Michigan. Originally issued in two
volumes. Reprinted in one volume.

A Bruccoli-Clark book
Copyright © 1972
The National Cash Register Company
Library of Congress Card Number:
72-76250
ISBN 0-910972-19-2

LETTERS OF

HAWTHORNE

TO WILLIAM D. TICKNOR

1851 – 1864

VOLUME I

NEWARK   NEW JERSEY
THE CARTERET BOOK CLUB
1910

FOREWORD

The chronicle of devoted friendship and business dependence in Nathaniel Hawthorne's letters to his publisher, William D. Ticknor, is the only authorial record of the autumn and winter of Hawthorne's career. Remarkable for its intimacy and detail, Hawthorne's 15-year correspondence with Ticknor provides insights into the mind and heart, as well as the activities, of the mature Hawthorne nowhere else available. To Ticknor, as to few others within his limited circle of trusted friends, Hawthorne freely divulged his feelings, his hopes, his needs, and his fears concerning his personal affairs. In Ticknor, Hawthorne found not only a staunch friend and good companion, but a financial counselor, banker, business advisor, traveling secretary, diplomatic courier, provisioner, broker, clerk, and publisher – for "Tick," as Hawthorne addressed him, served Hawthorne in all of these ways and more.

Hawthorne was 45, and William Davis Ticknor, the senior partner in Ticknor, Reed, and Fields, 39,[1] when, with the publication of *The Scarlet Letter* in the spring of 1850, Hawthorne's name was added to the firm's distinguished list of authors. This determination on the part of James T. Fields and William D. Ticknor to risk publishing the work of "the most unpopular writer in America," as Hawthorne over-modestly put it to Fields,[2] this willingness to gamble on native American literature, won for Ticknor and Fields Hawthorne's remaining literary productivity and enduring loyalty. *The Scarlet Letter* (1850) was followed by publication of seven new book-length works supplemented by various collections of Hawthorne's earlier writings. By 1854, four years after the commencement of their association, virtually the complete works of Hawthorne, with the exception of *The Marble Faun* (1860) and *Our Old Home* (1863), were available to the American reading public under a Ticknor, Reed, and Fields (later Ticknor and Fields) imprint. Their willingness to back an author in whom they believed was also the foundation for Hawthorne's lasting friendships with James T. Fields and William D. Ticknor. The Offices of Ticknor, Reed, and Fields at the time *The Scarlet Letter* appeared was the Old Corner Bookstore situated at the junction of Washington and School Streets in the heart of Boston. Since it also proved to be at the center of Boston literary life, the Old Corner Bookstore was dubbed Parnassus Corner in honor of the literary figures to be found within. As N. P. Willis reported to his *Home Journal* readers, "All our citizens will recognize the classic locality, happily termed 'Parnassus Corner', the bookstore of Messrs. Ticknor & Fields . . . Here congregates . . . a score of authors worth peeping at."[3] A few of those numbered among the host of Parnassus Corner regulars were Longfellow, Emerson, Lowell, Whittier, Holmes, Whipple, Agassiz, Thackeray, when he was in America, and, on numerous occasions before he left for Liverpool, Hawthorne. Although Hawthorne, as was his custom, proved more content to be an observer than a participant at the Parnassus literary court, he enjoyed his visits sufficiently to spend hours at a time, sitting by the side of his friend Ticknor.

Ticknor presided over the counting-room at the Old Corner Bookstore, an area elevated two or three steps above floor level. From this observation post, Ticknor could completely survey affairs in the store -- and it was here, in a somewhat secluded corner beside his desk, that he reserved a chair for Hawthorne. There was a little gate guarding the entrance into the counting-room which would have afforded Hawthorne's visits with Ticknor a measure of privacy without interfering with Hawthorne's observation of the goings-on in the store. When Hawthorne was lured out of his chair beside Ticknor's desk, it was to join a select gathering in Fields' green-curtained inner sanctum at the opposite corner of the shop, or to join one or both of the active partners for a short walk up School Street to the Parker House, or around the corner to Mrs. Haven's popular coffee-room.

In October of 1851, with *The Scarlet Letter* (1850), a new edition of *Twice-*

Told Tales (1851), and *The House of the Seven Gables* (1851), in print, James T. Fields left for England on a journey that was to last a year. Fields, who was instrumental in securing Hawthorne's work for publication by Ticknor, Reed, and Fields, had borne the primary responsibility for literary contact with the author, leaving most of the business details to Ticknor. Fields' extended stay abroad served to bring Hawthorne and Ticknor closer together as Hawthorne looked more and more to Ticknor for help and counsel. During Fields' absence, publication of *A Wonder Book* (1852), *The Snow-Image* (1852), *The Blithedale Romance* (1852), and Hawthorne's *Life of Franklin Pierce* (1852), was supervised by Ticknor. While Fields was successful in negotiating English rights for *Blithedale* – an admirable achievement in Hawthorne's view[4] – Ticknor became Hawthorne's principal business contact. Ticknor was of particular service in assisting Hawthorne with the delicate task of preparing, publishing, and promoting the campaign biography Hawthorne prepared for his old Bowdoin College friend, Franklin Pierce, who was running for the Presidency on the Democratic ticket in 1852. While Fields returned to Boston in time to help with certain aspects of distribution and promotion of the Pierce *Life*, it fell to Ticknor, a Whig, to make the arrangements with the Democratic Party for the purchase of 5,000 copies at, as Hawthorne proposed to Ticknor, "the most liberal terms you may be inclined to offer . . . " (2 October 1852). The sale was consumated at a 62-1/2% discount to Pierce's backers.[5] Ticknor was also asked by Hawthorne to maintain liaison with General Pierce in Hawthorne's behalf when Pierce's election to the Presidency carried with it the promise that the author could expect to be rewarded for his literary efforts on behalf of the candidate. Impatient regarding his prospects and petitioned for help by others who knew of his friendship with the new President, Hawthorne wrote Ticknor asking that he sound out Pierce on how the plans for Hawthorne were materializing: "Are you diplomatist enough to find out from the General whether he means to remove young Cass from the Roman chargeship? If you could do this before he leaves Boston, it would be doing me a great favor – not that I have anything personally to do with it. I should not like to have him know that I asked the question; but perhaps you might get the truth out of him by enquiring what he would give me, in case I did not go to Liverpool" (16 February 1853). Ticknor proved a sufficient "diplomatist" to warrant Hawthorne seeking his friend's valued services 10 days later when Ticknor was again asked to intervene with the President: "I enclose you a letter for the Emperor Frank, which I hope you will deliver in person, and follow up its arguments with any better ones that may occur to yourself" (26 February 1853). Pierce's appointment of Hawthorne to the Liverpool Consulship was confirmed by the Senate on 26 March 1853. When the news reached Hawthorne, he immediately wrote Ticknor to say that he now felt "rather inclined to follow up our idea of going to Washington in two or three weeks" (28 March 1853). Hawthorne, who had made a youthful prediction that Frank Pierce would become President, must have been pleased at the prospect of visiting his old college friend in the White House. Ticknor's business instincts must surely have been cordially disposed to the idea of White House connections, and plans were made for a joint trip. Both Hawthorne and Ticknor correctly felt there could be further personal advantage to be had from a Washington visit.

The Washington visit lasted more than two weeks and proved to be quite a social experience, with both Hawthorne and Ticknor receiving numerous invitations and an overwhelming amount of hospitality. In addition to social encounters, both Ticknor and Hawthorne had several private interviews each with the President. Ticknor wrote his wife that "I told the President that I had been unable to decide what to ask for, – but upon the whole would leave it for him to suggest some liberal 'gift.' He replied that he thought he had better exchange places with me. Believing my position to be the most agreeable. I, of course, declined. Hawthorne is quite a lion here. Much attention is shown, and yet it annoys him very much. He is to take tea with the President to-night" (22 April 1853).[6] Hawthorne benefited from the trip in a very material way, as

Ticknor also reported to his wife: "Hawthorne has accomplished a good deal for himself. In addition to the Liverpool Consulship he has secured the Manchester also, -- which adds to his income some $3,000 annually. This he would have lost, if he had not come on. I am very glad for his sake" (28 April 1853).[7]

In the two months following the Washington visit, Hawthorne had to prepare for the impending move to Liverpool. Adding to the confusion, was the uncertainty concerning all the arrangements that would have to be made in Liverpool. Once more, the faithful Ticknor found a way of aiding his friend Hawthorne. When the Cunard screw steamer *Niagara* sailed from Boston on 6 July 1853 taking the new American Consul and his family to Liverpool, Ticknor was also a passenger. As it had seemed a good idea to storm Washington together, it now seemed essential to get Hawthorne properly installed as Consul. Reporting to his wife, who had remained in Boston, Ticknor wrote that he had "remained with [Hawthorne] till Wednesday arranging his business as well as I could until he enters upon his duties August 1st.... In Liverpool there is not much to be seen except the Docks and their Commercial buildings. I would not have remained twelve hours, but for Hawthorne. He wished me to stay by him as long as possible" (22 July 1853).[8]

Throughout the term of his Consulship, and for all the years that Hawthorne was abroad, he continued to depend on Ticknor. The Ticknor-Hawthorne correspondence reveals the extent of this dependency in the many ways Ticknor managed to help Hawthorne, from uncomplainingly performing simple services to faithfully fulfilling the most important duties, responsibility for all of which Ticknor had seemingly gladly accepted as the basis of his friendship for his author-comrade. Whether it was seeing to the presentation copies of Hawthorne's latest work to be distributed, to the payment of an outstanding account, the repayment of a long-standing debt, supplying Hawthorne with an advance of funds, seeing to a case of claret or the tailor, or loaning money to one of Hawthorne's friends against his better judgment and the counsel he had given . Hawthorne, Ticknor was always faithful to the task. It was a code of friendship in which he was instructed by Hawthorne: ". . . as to your advice not to lend any more money, I acknowledge it to be good, and shall follow it so far as I can and ought. But when the friend of half my lifetime asks me to assist him, and when I have perfect confidence in his honor, what is to be done? Shall I prove myself to be one of those persons who have every quality desirable in friendship, except that they invariably fail you at the pinch? I don't think I can do that; but, luckily, I have fewer friends than most men, and there are not a great many who can claim anything of me on that score" (19 January 1855).

One final journey Ticknor made with his friend. In the Spring of 1864, at a time when Hawthorne's health had visibly failed, it was arranged that Ticknor would accompany Hawthorne south to see if in this way Hawthorne could regain his strength. The first leg of the journey took the travelers as far as New York, where they sought shelter from a violent storm. Knowing Mrs. Hawthorne's concern for her husband, Ticknor wrote to her from the Astor House, "It will take a few days to see what effect this change will have upon him; but I can't but hope that it will prove the right medicine . . . . I can only say that I hope the trip may accomplish what we all desire; and I have great faith" (30 March 1864).[9] The storm persisted, and Hawthorne and Ticknor remained trapped at the Astor House awaiting an improvement in traveling conditions. Again Ticknor reported to Mrs. Hawthorne: "I assure you he is much improved, but he is yet very weak. The weather has been as bad as possible, and of course we have not been out much. I intended to have left New York yesterday, but I thought it best not to leave in a driving storm . . . . I cannot say where we go next, as I shall be governed by what shall seem best for him" (3 April 1864).[10]

On 7 April, Ticknor wrote his wife that he and Hawthorne had arrived in Philadelphia, again in stormy weather. Although feeling unwell himself, his first thought was for Hawthorne "Excuse this short note, as I must look after my friend. I have a bad cold and feel disinclined to move at all" (7 April 1864).[11] On the following day, Ticknor was seriously ill, and Hawthorne suddenly found himself looking after his benefactor. On Sunday morning, 10 April 1864, Hawthorne was appalled by the death of his friend. For Hawthorne, Ticknor's death was a terrible loss under the most desperate circumstances. After making what arrangements were required, Hawthorne returned to Boston, where he stopped briefly to see Fields. By the time Hawthorne reached The Wayside in Concord, he was utterly shaken. The scene of his return is preserved in a letter from Mrs. Hawthorne to James T. Fields: "He came back unlooked-for that day; and when I heard a step on the piazza, I was lying on a couch and feeling quite indisposed. But as soon as I saw him, I was frightened out of all knowledge of myself, – so haggard, so white, so deeply scored with pain and fatigue was the face, so much more ill he looked than I ever saw him before. He had walked from the station because he saw no carriage there, and his brow was streaming with a perfect rain, so great had been the effort to walk so far . . . . He needed much to get home to me, where he could fling off all care of himself and give way to his feelings, pent up and kept back for so long, especially since his watch and ward of most excellent, kind Mr. Ticknor."[1][2]

Hawthorne's declining health was damaged by the shock of Ticknor's death, and on 19 May 1864, while on a trip in the company of General Pierce, Hawthorne passed away in his sleep in his room at the Pemigewasset House in Plymouth, New Hampshire.

C. E. Frazer Clark, Jr.

---

[1] Hawthorne was born in Salem, Massachusetts, 4 July 1804. Ticknor was born in Lebanon, New Hampshire, 6 August 1810.

[2] Hawthorne as quoted by James T. Fields in *Yesterdays With Authors* (Boston: Houghton, Mifflin, 1882), p. 49.

[3] W. S. Tryon, *Parnassus Corner* (Boston: Houghton Mifflin, 1963), p. 221.

[4] Hawthorne to Fields, 17 June 1852.

[5] Jacob Blanck, *Bibliography of American Literature* (New Haven and London: Yale University Press, 1963), Vol. IV, p. 12.

[6] Caroline Ticknor, *Hawthorne and His Publisher* (Boston and New York: Houghton Mifflin, 1913), p. 44.

[7] *Ibid.*, p. 46.

[8] *Ibid.*, p. 53.

[9] *Ibid.*, p. 314.

[10] *Ibid.*, p. 315.

[11] *Ibid.*, p. 320.

[12] *Yesterdays*, pp. 118-119.

INTRODUCTION

Nathaniel Hawthorne was born in Salem, Massachusetts, July 4, 1804, and lived there, save for a short stay in Maine during his fourteenth year, until he was twenty-nine. He took up literary work immediately after graduating from Bowdoin College in 1825, and writing was the one absorbing passion of his whole life. He was a wage earner in the Boston Custom House in 1839–41; joined the Brook Farm settlement in 1841; was in the Salem Custom House 1846–49; and was American consul at Liverpool 1853–57. He died in 1864. Of the thirty-nine years of his life after he left college, thirty were devoted almost entirely to literature. His novels, tales, and sketches form only a small part of his literary work. He filled many note-books with observations, comments, and reflections, most of which were written with a view to their publication. It was inevitable that one who had so constantly in mind the thought of literary production should display

his literary habit even in his intimate and familiar letters, and the letters included in these two
volumes have much of the flavor of his more
formal and premeditated work.

They were addressed to his friend and publisher, William D. Ticknor, between November
14, 1851, and March 18, 1864, and are 146 in
number. Most of them were written in Liverpool while Hawthorne was American consul
there, as already stated. Julian Hawthorne
published extracts from a few of them in an
article entitled "A Group of Hawthorne Letters," which appeared in Harper's Magazine for
March, 1904. Except for these extracts, none
of them have before appeared in print. They
include nearly all the letters which Hawthorne
wrote to Mr. Ticknor between the dates above
given.

For more than half a century Hawthorne has
retained his place among the few American
writers of the first rank. That fact is sufficient
excuse for the publication of these volumes.
The letters they contain are of interest and
value, first, to the student of Hawthorne, and,

next, to the student of social, economic, and political conditions in both England and America fifty years ago.

It would be easy to extend this introduction by adding to it interesting extracts from the letters; but to do so seems quite unnecessary. A few of the many noteworthy things to be found in them are these: Hawthorne's remark that America seen from England looked to him "infernally disagreeable," September 26, 1856; that he sympathized with no political party, but "hated them all," October 10, 1856; that he did not believe in Miss Bacon's Bacon-Shakespeare book, but found it "to possess very great merit," November 6, 1856; but "d——d hard reading," January 31, 1857; that he would like to spend the remainder of his days in England, though not as consul, January 2, 1857; that "there is nothing in this world so much like hell as the interior of an American (merchant) ship," January 31, 1857; that he found it easy enough to make a speech at a banquet where he was "cornered and *corned*," January 31, 1857; that he very frequently relieved penniless

Americans who were abroad, and always with an abounding faith that they would repay him, April 9, 1857, and elsewhere; that he found English governesses "ignorant and inefficient," July 30, 1857; that he was sorry Heenan, the American prize-fighter, did not win a decisive victory over his English opponent, April 19, 1860; and that, as the time of his home-coming drew near, he looked upon New England "quite as a Paradise," April 19, 1860.

These references merely suggest how many, varied, and interesting are the points on which Hawthorne touches in this long and intimate correspondence.   J. C. D.

Concord, June 18th. 1852.

Dear Dickinson,

Will you be so kind as
to hand the enclosed letter to
Fields? He tells me he has
succeeded in getting two hundred pounds for the romance.
It will come in good time; for
I shall have to draw pretty
freely with my bills for repairs
&c are settled.

Truly yours,
Nath'l Hawthorne.

LETTERS OF HAWTHORNE TO
WILLIAM D. TICKNOR

Lenox, Nov. 14th, 1851.

Dear Sirs,

My friend Bridge has been ordered to sea, and wishes, before his departure, to pay $500 which he owes me. As I have no present use for this money, I have requested him to pay it into your hands, where, if you please, it may remain until wanted, subject to my draft.

By the by, I find that I underestimated my expenses in getting away from this place, and must have $100 more. Will you be kind enough to send me that amount, as soon as possible, by another certificate of deposit, addressed to the *Pittsfield bank? I intend to leave here the latter part of next week.

Mr. Bridge will call on you and hand over the $500.

Truly yours,

Nath¹ Hawthorne.

*Agricultural Bank, Pittsfield.

Concord, June 8th, 1852.

Dear Ticknor,

We are established here; and Mrs. Hawthorne will be ready to hang up the portrait, whenever you shall be kind enough to send it.

I find myself surrounded with a host of carpenters, masons, &c: — each presenting a long bill. I have compounded with my creditors to pay them $100 in hand, and the rest at an early date. If convenient to you, I should like to have a certificate of deposit, or some other kind of draft, payable at the bank here, for the above sum.

I rec'd a note from Fields, informing me of his hopes of getting £200 for the romance. I don't believe he will.

Truly yours,

Nath¹ Hawthorne.

Concord, June 13th, 1852.

Dear Ticknor,

Will you be kind enough to send the package for Miss Cushman to No. 107, Washington street (J. F. Pray's shoe-store) as soon as possible. I take the liberty, although you are a bitter whig, to enclose a letter which I wish to be conveyed to Gen¹ Pierce; because it is of importance that it should reach him immediately, and were I to send by mail, I fear it will not reach him so soon. He intended to return to Boston on Monday (tomorrow) and I suppose will be at the Tremont. Possibly, they may keep him at home till Tuesday.

> Truly yours,
>
> Nath. Hawthorne.

> Concord, June 18th, 1852.

Dear Ticknor,

Will you be so kind as to send the enclosed letter to Fields? He tells me he has succeeded in getting two hundred pounds for the romance. It will come in good time; for I shall have to draw pretty freely till my bills for repairs &c are settled.

> Truly yours,
>
> Nath¹ Hawthorne.

Concord, July 13th, 1852.

Dear Ticknor,

I see you announce the book as to be published tomorrow. Please to send a copy to Mrs. Horatio Bridge, care of F. I. Bridge, Esq, Appraiser's Office, Custom House, Boston.

I am reduced to a penniless condition; and Mrs. Hawthorne, I believe, has thirteen cents in ready money. Please to send a small supply — say twenty-five dollars — as speedily as possible.

I make no progress with the biography, on account of the sluggishness of the people who ought to furnish the materials.

Truly yours,

Nath[l] Hawthorne.

Concord, July 24th, 1852.

Dear Ticknor,

I am glad you have got rid of so many of the new books. Sweep them off as fast as you can. Don't let your shelves be disgraced with such trash.

As for the biography, I have but just been supplied with the materials for commencing it.

I shall set to work to-morrow in good earnest, and shall not show my face till it is finished.

Your claret was most excellent and acceptable, and has already given me a great deal of comfort. Some other friends have sent me some sauterne, some champagne, and some sherry; and I have laid in a supply of first rate brandy on my own hook; so that I hope to keep myself pretty jolly, in spite of the Maine Law.

Fields writes me that he has sent two packages for me, by the same steamer that brought his letter. Did they arrive?

Truly yours,

Nath¹ Hawthorne.

Concord, Oct. 2d, '52.

Dear Ticknor,

Mr. Augustus Schell (who calls himself "Ch. Dem. Rep. Gen. Com.ᵉᵉ") has written to me about the Life of Pierce. His committee wish for license to print an edition of the book for gratuitous circulation in the city of New York; and he says he has addressed you on the same subject. For my own part, I should be in favor of granting the largest liberty, and shall willingly accede to the most liberal terms you may be inclined to offer him. I don't believe it would essentially injure the circulation to let him print five thousand in a cheap style, *gratis*. But do just as you like; and pray don't let me hear any more of it.

Yours truly, Nath. Hawthorne.

Concord, Jany 21st, '53.

Dear Ticknor,

I thank you heartily for those cigars. They will keep your memory fragrant for many a day to come.

The account arrived today. I am glad to see so good a balance to my credit. It will diminish fast enough.

Could you ask Healy on what day it would be convenient to have me sit? I don't think Mrs. Hawthorne will be able to come again— she being quite ill of influenza.

Yours truly,

Nath. Hawthorne.

Concord, Feb. 16th, 1853.

Dear Ticknor,

Are you diplomatist enough to find out from the General whether he means to remove young Cass from the Roman charge-ship? If you could do this before he leaves Boston, it would be doing me a very great favor—not that I have anything personally to do with it. I should not like to have him know that I asked the question; but perhaps you might get the truth out of him by enquiring what he would give me, in case I did not go to Liverpool.

The fact is, I have a friend, who wishes to apply for it, in case Cass is to be removed.

Very truly yours,

N. H.

Concord, Feb. 26th, 1853.

Dear Ticknor,

I enclose you a letter for the Emperor Frank, which I hope you will deliver in person, and follow up its arguments with any better

ones that may occur to yourself. For this purpose, I have sent it unsealed.

I rather think you had better not show it to
Colonel Miller — not that I care much about it,
either way; but it was not written for his eye.

I trust you will go to Washington. You
ought to be seeing about the red tape and
wrapping-paper. You might help Colonel
Miller, and very probably, do me a good turn
into the bargain. The General means well;
but it would be a great pity if he should be led
into doing a wrong thing as regards that consulship.

Truly yours,

N. H.

Concord, March 15th, '53.

Dear Ticknor,

I send the Tanglewood Tales. According to
my calculation, they will make rather less than
300 pages, containing the same number of
lines as the pages of the Wonder Book. I
wish you would send it to press immediately,
and have the illustrations done after it is *printed;*

otherwise, I may not be able to correct the proofs.

Yours truly,

N. H.

Concord, March 28th, 1853.

Dear Ticknor,

The President has made the appointment; but it is not to take effect until the first of August — my predecessor having resigned, but wishing to retain his position till that date.

I feel rather inclined to follow out our idea of going to Washington in two or three weeks. My best dress-coat is rather shabby (befitting an author much more than a man of consular rank); so, when you next smoke a cigar with our friend Driscoll, I wish you would tell him to put another suit on the stocks for me — a black dress-coat and pantaloons; and he may select the cloth. I shall want them before we go to Washington.

Perhaps I may be in Boston in the course of the week — perhaps not.

Truly yours,

Nath¹ Hawthorne.

Concord, April 1st, 1853.

Dear Ticknor,

If Mr. Burchmore should inquire for me at the Bookstore, please to tell him that I have something of importance to communicate about his affairs, and that I think it desirable he should see me before going to Salem. If he calls in the morning, he might take the noon-train; otherwise, he must come and stay all night.

Yours truly,

Nath¹ Hawthorne.

Concord, June 20th, 1853.

Dear Ticknor,

I am to have somebody at dinner to-morrow. Will you order me half a dozen of good claret, and have it sent by Adams' Express to-night. If you will come here, this week or next, and drink half of it yourself, you may send a whole dozen; — otherwise six bottles are as much as I can get rid of. I will settle for it when I come — which will be in a day or two.

Truly yours,

Nath¹ Hawthorne.

Concord, July 5th, 1853.

Gentlemen,

You are hereby authorized to pay and charge to my account the drafts of my sister, Elizabeth M. Hawthorne, to an amount not exceeding two hundred dollars per annum, during my absence in Europe. Truly yours,

Nath¹ Hawthorne.

Messrs Ticknor, Reed, & Fields,
Boston.

Liverpool, July 22d, 1853.

Dear Ticknor,

I have this moment rec'd yours of yesterday, and I suppose, before this time, you have mine of same date. In reference to the subject of the letter, I am happy to say that Mr. Ingersoll rec'd my commission by the Baltic; and that the Exequatur will immediately be put upon it.

We have had very dull times here since you left us; and to tell you the truth, I believe we are all very homesick. Mrs. Blodgett cannot receive us till next Wednesday. The children find the hotel a veritable prison. As for my-

self, I have had but little enjoyment in a
solitary cigar, and seldom feel like visiting a
beer-shop, without your countenance. I wish
I could come to London, but consider it unad-
visable at present, for several reasons.

My wife, just now, has gone out to walk
with the children or she would certainly send
you her warmest remembrances; — so would
Una, Julian, and Rosebud, who all miss you
more than they would their father. Ellen and
Mary (especially the former) have also con-
ceived a great regard for you.

I send the assignment on the opposite half
sheet.

With my best regards to Grace, and likewise
to Mr. Bennoch —

Your friend,

Nath¹ Hawthorne.

Liverpool, July 30th, 1853.

Dear Ticknor,

If I remember right, there were but 336
pages in your edition of "Tanglewood," and I

am sure the last story ends with a sentence about the departure of the Argonauts after obtaining the Golden Fleece — Orpheus playing on his harp, and the vessel skimming over the water. I left the conclusion to the readers' imagination. I have not the book at hand to refer to.

My engagements are such that I can't possibly come to London on the day named by Mr. Bennoch. I wish I could; but it will be just at the beginning of my administration, and it will never do for me to run away at once.

We did not get to Mrs. Blodgett's till Thursday; and I assure you we were all heartily sick of the Hotel — nor shall we feel at our ease until settled in a house which we can, temporarily, call our own. I have found very little enjoyment, thus far, in my visit to England.

I long to see you.

> Truly yours,
>
> Nath¹ Hawthorne.

Liverpool, August 22d, 1853.

Dear Ticknor,

I have engaged berth No. 37 for you, in steamer Niagara, to sail September 3d. . . . . No. 37 is situated just about the same as the one you came over in.

If you have time, before leaving London, I wish you would buy a lady's watch, good and handsome, but not very expensive — sufficiently so, however, to ensure a faithful time-keeper. Are there any objections to Swiss watches? Ladies' watches, I believe, are not so costly as gentlemen's; and I should suppose that ten or twelve guineas might fetch a good one.

Do Chapman and Hall mean to send me any copies of "Tanglewood"?

If you want money before sailing, I can let you have £50 or thereabouts — perhaps more. I have had to pay for the furniture of the office, and other preliminary expenses; so that there is less on hand than would otherwise have been the case.

Do try to spend two or three days here, before sailing. I shall feel as if my last friend was leaving me, when you go aboard. You had better come to the Rock Ferry Hotel, whence you can be transferred to the steamer.

Dr. Bailey and wife are now here, intending to sail on Wednesday.

Truly yours,

Nath¹ Hawthorne.

P. S. Drive at once from the railway down to the Rock Ferry steamer, at George's Dock. It goes every half-hour through the day, and until ten o'clock p.m. Mrs. Hawthorne and the children will not excuse you, if you do not come.

Liverpool, August 24th, 1853.

Dear Ticknor,

Could not the white-faced watch be bought, with the understanding that it might be exchanged for a gold-faced one, in case the latter should be preferred? And you might select also the gold-faced one, to be sent if I return the white-face. Do you mean to bring the watch, or send it? I don't care which.

I think I had better not come to London yet.

I shall probably have £100 for you; perhaps more. The gold begins to chink.

Truly yours,

Nath¹ Hawthorne.

Liverpool, August 25th, 1853.

Dear Ticknor,

I have transferred you to berth No. 58, steamer America, to sail September 17th. Before that time, if I mistake not, we shall be established in a house of our own at Rockferry; so that you will find yourself at home here. The steamers anchor within two or three hundred yards of us; and you can be put on board from our side of the river.

I like the watch much, and mean to keep it, if my wife approves of it as I do. I am very glad you bought it of Mr. Bennett, because his name gives assurance of its quality. Pay him; and I will fill your pockets when you go home.

Yours truly,

N. H.

Liverpool, Sept. 2d, 1853.

Dear Ticknor,

You must not think of going anywhere else than to our house. We got into it yesterday, and are just as well established as if we had been there a year. It is an abundantly large house, and we want you to let our American friends know, from your own experience, how comfortably we are situated. When you get to Liverpool, drive to the consulate, and I will cross the river with you; or, if I should not be at hand, you will easily find the way alone. The boats go half-hourly from George's Dock. Can't you come before the 14th?

Truly yours,

Nath¹ Hawthorne.

Should you have any difficulty in finding the house, inquire at the Rockferry Hotel — where we are well known.

Liverpool, Sept. 7th, 1853.

Dear Ticknor,

I don't believe you ever mean to go home at all. However, I am willing you should stay in England four years longer, at least; and so I have engaged a berth for you on the steamer of October 1st. In requital for my trouble, I shall expect you to spend a good deal of the intervening time with us. By the by, Julian wants to go home with you.

Truly yours,

Nath¹ Hawthorne.

Liverpool, Sept. 10th, '53.

Dear Ticknor,

Colonel Lawrence has forwarded a passport for you as bearer of despatches per steamer of Sept. 17th. As I have booked you for October 1st, you had better call at the Legation and state the fact, so that you may get the appointment for that date — provided you think it desirable.

The children long to see you; — so do Mrs. Hawthorne and myself.

> Truly yours,
>> Nath¹ Hawthorne.

> Liverpool, October 8th, '53.

Dear Tick —

While I write this, you are tossing in mid-ocean; but I hope it will find you safely ensconced in your Paradise, at the old corner. We all miss you very much.

Should my tax-bill for Concord be presented to you, please to pay it — or refund the money to Mr. Ball, if he pays it. We forgot to draw up the power of attorney; but I will send it, if you will instruct me how.

I wish you would send me two or three copies of Tanglewood; for Chapman has sent only one — and I want to give it to one or two friends.

Mrs. Hawthorne will buy some of those gloves as soon as the weather permits her to cross the river. I am looking out for a good cheese and some ale. Any further orders we shall be happy to execute. Talking of ale, I have hardly tasted that or any other liquor since you left us. I do need somebody to drink with, now and then. Englishmen are not to be trusted, to that extent. I dined with two of the sons of Burns, last Saturday, and got into great favor with them — partly by the affection which I showed for the whisky-bottle. One of them (an old white-headed major) sang several of his father's songs.

Send Fields over as soon as possible.

N. H.

Liverpool, Nov. 11th, '53.

Dear Ticknor,

I send two second bills of Exchange on the Secretary of State — the first having been sent by the last steamer. Also, three pairs of No. 7 gloves for yourself. Mrs. Hawthorne has been unable to find any of No. 6.

I received your note, and the copies of

Tanglewood, and am glad to hear that you are going to republish the True Stories. I don't remember any corrections to be made, and would rather spare myself the trouble and weariness of looking through the book. Let it go as it is.

The newspapers were very acceptable — being the first I had seen from Boston. I get New York papers in abundance.

We are all comfortably well.

With regards to Fields and other friends,

Truly yours,

N. Hawthorne.

Liverpool, Nov. 18th, '53.

Dear Ticknor,

You may draw for £250, which I shall deposit immediately to the credit of Tick. Reed & Fields.

Nothing new.

Yours truly,

N. H.

Liverpool, Nov. 25th, 1853.

Dear Ticknor,

I have to-day deposited with Baring Brothers three hundred pounds (£300) to the credit of Ticknor, Reed, & Fields. It will probably be the last deposit for some time; as next month's income will go to the payment of Christmas bills. I wish to Heaven I had made up my whole pile, and were off to Italy. I am tired of these English fogs.

Yours by the Niagara was received; as also the newspapers. Mrs. Hawthorne has been scolding me daily, since you went away, for not buying you a cheese; and I really meant to have sent one by this steamer; but have neglected it, such is the continual pressure and hurry and urgency of my business. When I have a moment to breathe, I will buy both the cheese and ale. I am almost worn out with hard work. In fact, you must have noticed how overburthened I was with consular engagements, while you were here. But I think I shall live through it.

What has become of Fields? He never

writes; and your own notes are of the briefest.
Can I do anything for you here?—or for any
of my friends or yours?

We are all as well as this abominable climate
will let us be. You speak of the "wretched
climate" of New England. God forgive you!
You ought to spend a November in England.

Truly yours,

Nath¹ Hawthorne.

P. S. My clerk says that Baring insists that
he has your special direction for calling your
firm W. D. Ticknor & Co. As he is so very
positive, I have told him to credit the money
thus, instead of to Ticknor, Reed, & Fields.
Tell me how it ought to be.

N. H.

Liverpool, Dec. 8th, 1853.

Dear Ticknor,

I enclose a small draft, drawn by an old
gentleman whose funds failed him here, and
whom I have had to assist and send home —
as I am compelled to do in many other cases,
at my own risk. He is now on his passage to

Philadelphia, by a screw-steamer. I think the draft will prove a good one; although my clerks (who have seen a thousand such cases) tell me that it will never be paid. In that event, I shall lose not only this, but a much larger sum for his passage-money.

I wish you would go to Mr. F. C. Butman, and learn what are the probabilities of William Lilley's draft on him being paid by said Lilley's friends. This fellow is a newly appointed consul to Pernambuco, and drew a bill on Butman for which I engaged to be responsible to Brown & Shipley, who advanced the money—£50. It turns out that he had no funds in Butman's hands, nor any right whatever to draw on him. If I lose the money, he shall lose his consulship; although I don't know that he is worse than many other of our foreign appointments, who are (but don't whisper it) a set of swindlers generally. They almost always get short of money here, and never can raise a shilling without my endorsement; for the Liverpool merchants seem to know their character of old. You must not take the above as true to the letter; though it has a great deal more truth in it than I wish it had.

I received an immense bale of newspapers by the last steamer, and thank you heartily for them. Bennoch and William [surname indecipherable] spent last two days with me. I had not time to do much for them in the way of an elaborate dinner; but I had a pleasant time, and I hope *they* did.

I suppose Baring Brothers have already advised you of my depositing £300 to your credit. If it had been £3000, I would kick the office to the devil, and come home again. I am sick of it, and long for my hillside; and — what I thought I never should long for — my pen! When once a man is thoroughly imbued with ink, he never can wash out the stain.

I am invited to dine with the mayor again, but don't mean to go.

Remember me to Fields, Whipple, Longfellow, and friends generally. I was delighted with Whipple's notice of Tanglewood.

> Truly yours,
>
> Nathl Hawthorne.

P. S. You had better send Mr. Hulm's letter to Daniel Winslow a day or two before you send the draft for collection.

N. H.

Liverpool, Jan. 6th, 1854.

Dear Ticknor,

I send the power of attorney with the mayor's seal and signature, and likewise my own consular certificate. I am quite at a loss how to get the regular two-dollar fee for this latter, unless *you* pay it. It is against all rule, to give it for nothing. However, as it is not likely to happen again, I will consent to lose the money, for this once.

I forwarded your package to Trübner, along with the Government bag. Grace's book, I suppose, is a republication of her letters to the Era; and, in that case, you will not make a fortune out of them. I am getting sick of Grace. Her "Little Pilgrim" is a humbug, and she herself is—but there is no need of telling you. I wish her well, and mean to write an article for her, by and by. But ink-stained women are, without a single exception, detestable.

I meant to have sent you that cheese by tomorrow's steamer, but have not had time to select a good one. You shall have it by the next one — or else I will give you leave to call me inattentive and unpunctual. The ale shall follow in due course. We must let it ripen a little, first.

Tell Colonel Miller that his friend Miss Cushman dined and spent the night with me (that is, in my house,) and that my wife and myself enjoyed her society very much. She spoke with great interest of him; and we both wished that he could have been sitting at our English fireside.

I shall deposit £200 or £250 to your credit, before you receive this. You may draw with perfect certainty for the lesser sum.

Truly yours,

Nath¹ Hawthorne.

Liverpool, Feb. 3d, 1854.

Dear Ticknor,

I send a note from Una, thanking you, I presume, for your magnificent present of paper.

I have been very busy lately with those shipwrecked vagabonds from the San Francisco—having had to clothe and feed them all on my own private responsibility. Uncle Sam will pay me, I suppose, and he will likewise pay a larger sum for their passage home than all their bodies and souls are worth. I made the bargain myself; so you will readily conclude that it was a poor one. This responsibility, however, rests on the shoulders of the officer commanding—not on mine.

I have deposited £310 (three hundred & ten pounds) to your credit with the Barings.

If you know of any American Gazeteer, cheap and accurate, and of recent date, I wish you would send me a copy per next despatch. So many inquiries are made of me with respect to American localities, that I need something of the kind; but if not very recently published, there is no use in sending it.

I have paid Lilley's protested bill, some time ago, and have drawn upon him for the amount and damages, at three days' sight. In my letter of advice, I gave him to understand what my course will be, in case he does not honor the draft.

I sent your cheese per last steamer. Sometime or other, you shall have the ale.

As usual, I had something else to say, but have forgotten it.

Truly yours,

Nath¹ Hawthorne.

Liverpool, Feb. 17th, '54.

Dear Tick —

Thank you for the books and papers. Those are admirable poems of Mrs. Howe's, but the devil must be in the woman to publish them. It seems to me to let out a whole history of domestic unhappiness. What a strange propensity it is in these scribbling women to make a show of their hearts, as well as their heads, upon your counter, for anybody to pry into

that chooses! However, I, for one, am much
obliged to the lady, and esteem her beyond all
comparison the first of American poetesses.
What does her husband think of it?

I notified you in my last that I had deposited
£310 to your credit with the Barings. The
box is getting heavy again, and I shall soon
deposit two or three hundred more. Now that
business is becoming brisk, it will be sufficiently
safe for you to draw upon the Barings at any
time for £200, giving me one steamer's notice.
I ought to deposit at least that sum every five
weeks; but I rather prefer to wait till it reaches
£300.

Redding has published a list of the monied
men of Massachusetts. I consider myself one
of them, since you tell me I have $3000 safely
invested. Send me the pamphlet; for I ought
to be acquainted with the names of my brethren.

I think I have asked you for a United States
Gazeteer.

That must have been a glorious dinner at the
Cornhill Coffee House.

Fields' friend Miss Glynn is in Liverpool,

and Bennoch has sent me a letter of introduction to her. I shall probably deliver it, although rather shy of actresses.

We are all well.

Truly yours,   **N. H.**

Please to pay Driscoll's bill, and remember me to him. I wish I had got him to make me a consular dress; for it would have been first-rate to wear to a fancy-ball, to which I am invited to-night. Having nothing to wear, I shan't go.

N. H.

Liverpool, March 3d, '54.

Dear Tick —

Draw for £370 (three hundred and seventy pounds) this day deposited to your credit with the Barings. With my last deposit, this makes £680 since the first of January. Invest — invest — invest! I am in a hurry to be rich enough to get away from this dismal and forlorn hole. If I can once see $20,000 in a pile, I shan't care much for being turned out of office; and yet I ought to be a little richer than that. It won't be quite so easy for us to live on a thousand dollars, or less, as it used to be. I am getting spoilt, you see.

I forget (as usual) something that I wanted to say.

Truly yours,

Nath¹ Hawthorne.

United States Consulate,
Liverpool, March 30th, 1854.

Dear Ticknor,

I enclose a paragraph from the Marblehead Advocate, defending me, in my official capacity, from a statement in the Portsmouth Journal relative to my conduct with regard to the San Francisco sufferers. If nothing further has been said of the affair, let it rest. It will not be worth while to rake up a forgotten slander. But I herewith send you the facts of the case, to be used if necessary.

When Captain Watkins and Lieutenant Winder came to my office, I explained to them that I was not officially empowered to provide for sending the troops home, but that I would telegraph to Mr. Buchanan, and ascertain whether he would take the direction of the affair, or sanction my proceedings in it. This appeared to me the most eligible course, because his larger powers would probably enable him to do everything that was necessary; and also because (not being empowered to pledge the Government credit, and my private means being very limited) I doubted whether it would be possible for me to charter a steamer or other vessel, without the minister's sanction. Mr. Buchanan replied to my message, that he had no authority to take charge of the troops; neither did he offer any advice as to my own course; but he facilitated my operations by suggesting to Messrs. Baring Brothers to open a credit with me in behalf of the San Francisco sufferers. I do not question the propriety of Mr. Buchanan's conduct and am bound to presume that he could estimate the extent of his official powers better than I could do it for him.

Before Mr. Buchanan's answer was received, Captain Watkins had started for London, not by my request or advice, but solely for his own satisfaction. Meanwhile, I had given directions for supplying the troops with provisions and clothing, on my personal credit, and to the amount of about two thousand dollars — that being the extent of Lieutenant Winder's requisition. This was the only part of the business in which I used the services of my clerk; he being well acquainted with the quality and prices of the articles required. Before the answer was received, too, I had begun to seek for the means of transportation; and before noon of the day after the arrival of the troops, I had four propositions from ship-owners ready for the commanding officer's consideration. Mr. Buchanan had nothing whatever to do with the matter; neither had Captain Watkins, who did not return from London until after the arrangements were made. Lieutenant Winder, as commander of the detachment, signed the contract for the charter of the steamer; and I, as consul, appended my official certificate of his competency so to do.

I cannot imagine who is the author of the false statement to which I have referred. Certainly it could not have been either Captain Watkins or Lieutenant Winder, from neither of whom did I hear a word of complaint or dissatisfaction; and after parting from me in perfect kindness, and with thanks for my services, they are not the men to attack me behind my back, on the other side of the Atlantic, and anonymously, through a newspaper. Yet no other person, except those two, is qualified to give any account of the matter.

The above comprises all that I need say. You will observe that I was no more bound by my official instructions to take charge of these men, to feed and clothe them, or to send them home, than any private citizen would have been. But I should never dream of taking any credit to myself for my doings in the matter. I did nothing more than was virtually and morally, though not officially, incumbent on me. Any man of common sense and common feeling would have seen (as I saw) that his duty, in such a position as mine, must be measured by the peculiar exigencies of the case and by his utmost capacity to deal with them and not by the narrow letter of his instructions, which were framed to meet only the ordinary routine of events. I therefore claim no praise. But, on the other hand, I certainly deserve no censure; for my duty, on the largest interpretation of its limits, was as amply and as promptly performed as if I had been clothed with the fullest official powers for this identical contingency.

Truly yours,

Nath[l] Hawthorne.

P. S. I was ready to sign the contract as principal, had the agent of the Cunard line preferred that course; but, instead of the Government credit, it would have involved merely my personal liability, which was very inadequate to the occasion. During the progress of the negotiation, if I mistake not, a despatch had been received by Lieutenant Winder from the Secretary of War, expressly authorizing him to charter a steamer or other vessel for the transportation of the troops.

Do not make this public, unless circumstances imperatively demand it. Otherwise, put it by.

N. H.

Liverpool, April 7th, '54.

Dear Ticknor,

I send three 2d bills of exchange on the Secretary of State — the three firsts having been sent by the last Boston steamer. I also transmit a first bill for $29.83 — which please to get negotiated.

In my last (among various other matters, of more or less importance) I mentioned that Bridge wished to borrow $3000. Including the bills now sent, I shall probably be able to put that amount to your credit within three months; so that, unless he needs it before that time, it would not be necessary to disturb any good investment which you may have already made. But consult his convenience on this point, and do not let him hear of any difficulty.

You will be quite safe in drawing on the Barings for £200, as I have that amount now ready to deposit. I shall most probably make it up to £250; and if your understanding with them is such that they will not object to a possible overdrawal for so small an amount, you had better make the draft for the latter sum.

Would not North (our Washington friend) be able to exert some influence with regard to the invoice-business, mentioned in my last? It is really a matter of importance.

Give my regards to all friends, and believe me

Yours truly,

Nath¹ Hawthorne.

Liverpool, April 30th, '54.

Dear Ticknor,

I send a pamphlet which I have been requested to forward to the Professor of Mineralogy at Cambridge. I don't know who he is,— so must leave it to you.

There is no news here worth telling you. We are expecting the arrival of the Collins steamer,

which is now several days behind her time.
Mr. Buchanan has been here since Tuesday in
expectation of his niece, who is supposed to be
on board the steamer. I had the old fellow
to dine with me, and liked him better than I
expected; so I hope you have not found
it necessary to publish my letter on the San
Francisco business; for though I made it bear
lightly on him, it would undoubtedly have pro-
voked a feud between us. But he takes his
wine like a true man, loves a good cigar, and
is doubtless as honest as nine diplomatists out
of ten.

My friend O'Sullivan and his family have
been staying with me, this past fortnight, on
their way to Portugal.

The circular of the Secretary of the Treasury,
to which you allude, is I suppose the same
about which I have already written you. It
will seriously affect the emoluments of the
office; but, if nothing worse happens, I shall
still get rather more than my $20,000 out of it.
The truth is, it is a devilish good office; — if
those jackasses at Washington (of course, I do

not include the President under this polite phrase) will but let it alone. They are now tinkering at a bill involving the whole subject of diplomatic and consular emoluments; and if they touch the Liverpool consulate at all, it will be to limit it by a salary. Now, with the inevitable expenses of a residence here, a salary of ten thousand dollars would hardly make it worth my while to keep the office — and they would never think of giving more than six. But, I trust in God, Pierce will not let them meddle with me.

Before this reaches you, Fields will have sailed for England. I shall be rejoiced to see him, and shall make him come at once to my house. I wish I could hope to see you along with him.

Truly yours,

Nath¹ Hawthorne.

Liverpool, May 5th, '54.

Dear Ticknor,

Three or four weeks since, I told you that you might draw for £200 or £250. I have this day deposited with the Barings £335 (three hundred and thirty-five pounds) so that there will be a considerable surplus over the largest of the above amounts. Business seems to have slackened a good deal; but I hope to be able to make up the rest of Bridge's $3000 in the course of a few weeks more. In the meantime, do not let him be put to any inconvenience; for he has been a true friend to me, when friends were few.

I hope Emery will be able to effect something as regards the Invoice certificates, but don't much expect it.

I am glad you did not find it necessary to publish my defence on the San Francisco business; for it is humiliating to be compelled to stand before the public in an attitude of defence. And, besides, I should have made several enemies — which it is not desirable to do, except in case of necessity. But *somebody* must have lied most damnably.

Truly yours,

Nathl Hawthorne.

Liverpool, May 12th, '54.

Dear Ticknor,

Per last New York steamer, I advised you of a deposit of £335 with the Barings.

I thank you heartily for your kind exertions in regard to the Invoice certificates. I can think of nothing to add to my arguments; except that, by dispensing with the certificates, a great injury is done to Americans (viz: myself and all the other consuls in England, Scotland, and Ireland) for the sake of conferring a miserable little favor and facility on Englishmen and Canadians, who will never thank us for it, and who will abuse their opportunities to defraud the revenue, if they can. It is a piece of unmitigated folly, which old Guthrie ought to be ashamed of. If he knew the character of English merchants as well as I begin to know it, he would see the expediency of creating new checks against their malfeasances, instead of relaxing any old ones. I have been quite surprised to find that our respectable merchants have a higher moral standard than the same class of men here. We Americans are the best people in the world,—but it is a poor world at that.

I sent you a fortnight ago, a small pamphlet on Crystallography. Did I say that it was intended for the Professor of Mineralogy at Cambridge?

It gratifies me much to see that you have been presented with an elegant silver tea-service. I hope to take a cup of tea from that silver tea-pot, some evening or other.

My wife is pretty well, and the children quite hearty. As for myself, I am afraid (from the compliments which I receive about my healthy aspect) that I am getting a little too John Bull-ish, and must diminish my allowance of roast beef, brown-stout, port, and sherry. I never felt better in my life. England is certainly the country to eat in, and to drink in.

Remember me to Col. Miller, and thank him for his letter to the Department about the Invoice Certificates, and also for the Salem Gazettes—which, by the by, did not come per last steamer.

I shall be rejoiced to see Fields, and will

send him home in August according to your
directions — if I can catch him.

Truly yours,

Nath¹ Hawthorne.

Liverpool, June 7th, 1854.

Dear Ticknor,

You put me to my trumps by asking for
additional matter for the "Mosses"; for I considered myself exhausted on that score, long
ago. Nevertheless, there is "Feathertop" —
which is almost as good as any of them. Let
that go in. It has just occurred to me, moreover, that in the New England Magazine, when
published by Park Benjamin, many of the
stories appeared which are now collected in the
"Twice-told Tales"; and the publication of
them was commenced with about ten or more
pages of introductory matter, which I think,
will do very well to publish as an article in the
"Mosses." It should be separated from all
extraneous stuff (which, if I recollect rightly,
may be done easy enough,) and may be called

"passages from a relinquished work "— or something of that kind. I believe the title was
"The Itinerant Storyteller." There are other
detached passages of mine, scattered through
Park Benjamin's volumes of that magazine;
and Fields would readily recognize them. Let
him do as he pleases about inserting any or all
of them; — only being careful to put in nothing
that he does not feel absolutely certain about.
The beginning, and the conclusion, of the
"Itinerant Storyteller" are there at an interval
of some months and are written quite up to the
usual level of my scribblings. If I had the
magazine at hand, I could patch up an article
in five minutes; and Fields can do it just as
well, and without any trouble at all. If he
should already have sailed, Whipple will doubtless do it. Do not put the patched up article
at the end of the volume, but somewhere about
the middle, where it will not attract so much
notice.

I am glad Bridge has the money. There is
nobody else (unless it were Pierce himself) to
whom I should feel obliged to lend any consid-

erable sum, as a matter of friendship. As regards future applications for loans, I shall refer them to you, and have them treated according to the principles of business. I must not forget to tell you that Lilly (the Pernambuco consul) has refunded the £50. I drew on him, and hinted pretty strongly, in my letter of advice, that he must pay the draft, on penalty of being reported to the State Department. I suffer constantly from beggars and borrowers to the amount of from one to five or ten pounds. This is unavoidable in my position, and must be looked upon as a necessary expense of the office; but beyond this I do not go.

In two or three weeks, I shall send you bills on the State Department, to the amount, I think, of above $1500. I shall fairly bag $10,000 within the year; and my expenses have been very heavy, too. I am terribly afraid Congress will cut down the office with a salary—in which case, it will not be worth holding. If I can have the full swing of the emoluments for one more year, I shall not grumble much; though (to tell you the truth)

I do not see how it will be possible for me to live, hereafter, on less than the interest of $40,000. I can't imagine how I ever did live on much less than that. It takes at least $100,000 to make a man quite comfortable — don't you think so? — and even then he would have to deny himself a great many very desirable things. To sum up the matter, I shall try to be content with a little, but would far rather have a great deal.

Yesterday I received a package, which appeared to be the one which you sent by the Andes. There being no bearer of despatches to take charge of it, it had been sent to the Custom House, and had lain there ever since, until inquiry was made on my part. They have overhauled it, and made me pay duty on the books which it contained, and postage on the letters. Among other books, there was a Gazeteer, which I sent for so long ago that I had forgotten it, but am very glad to get it now. Also, Grace Greenwood's Haps and Mishaps, which, it appears, she wishes to present to the Queen. I have forwarded it to Mr. Buchanan, who may hand it to her Majesty, if he chooses to make such a fool of himself.

It is best never to send a package, unless in charge of a bearer of despatches; and Mr. Glen would greatly oblige me by requesting the bearer to pay particular attention to the package. It should always accompany the despatch-bag, when the latter is brought on shore; otherwise it runs the risk of being sent to the Custom House, and causing me a good deal of trouble and expense. The bearer of despatches should consider it a part of his duty (as it really is) to deliver it; and he can do so without any additional trouble to himself.

Truly your friend,

Nath¹ Hawthorne.

P. S. All that I now recollect of my articles in the New England Magazine are,—The Storyteller aforesaid, begun in an early number and concluded long afterwards, I think, under some other title; and a description of an evening at the mountain-house, among the White Hills. These passages formed part of a work, the whole of which was never published. Do not print any more of it than will be sufficient to meet the exigency of the case; though really, as far as I can remember, it is no bad stuff.

U. S. Consulate,
Liverpool, June 16th, 1854.

Dear Ticknor,

I send two first bills of exchange on the Secretary of State for £24, 0, 4, and for £331, 7, 1. Get these cashed, and make a good use of the proceeds. I could not possibly live in this infernal hole, if it were not for the pleasure of occasionally sending you a thousand or two of dollars. I think I am quite up to the $10,000 mark now.

Truly yours,

Nath¹ Hawthorne.

Liverpool, June 23d, '54.

Dear Ticknor,

I have been greatly disappointed in not seeing Fields, but am glad to hear from some of his shipmates that they did not consider him in a dangerous condition. I shall hope for his arrival by the Niagara.

No package from you has come to hand by the America; but Mr. Beck told me that the bearer of despatches had charge of a box directed to me; and on inquiring what may have become of it, I find that the Custom House officers have seized it. They opened it, it appears, and found various dutiable articles, and, at the very bottom of the box, a quantity of cigars — too large a quantity to pass free of duty, and too small to be imported on paying duties. Nothing less, I think, than 100 lbs. weight is allowed to be entered. This is a very awkward occurrence; for it is now impossible to get the box, even by payment of fines and duties, without a special order from the Treasury in London; and it is by no means certain that this can be obtained. As respects the other articles, I shall do my best; for I understand from Mr. Beck that they were intended as presents for some of Fields' friends in London and elsewhere. As to the cigars, I have no hope of getting them out of limbo, and, indeed, do not think it advisable to make any strong attempt to do so, lest it should be supposed that I had some previous knowledge of the attempt to smuggle them. Even as the case stands, my consular good name can hardly fail to suffer some damage; and I am afraid the officers will pay special attention to all packages directed to me, hereafter. It was an ill-advised affair; but perhaps, when Fields arrives, he may be able to make such explanations as may facilitate the release of all except the cigars. They are gone to Hell; — and may the Devil smoke them!

My whole family (including my wife, and, I believe, myself) are at this moment in the spasmodic stage of the hooping-cough. The children have it pretty severely, but seem now to be on the mending point. This climate (as I have said a thousand times) is most detestable. We still find it necessary to keep fires.

I send two second bills of exchange on the Secretary of State; — the two firsts went by the last Cunard steamer to New York.

All Fields' friends appear to be in eager ex-
pectations of his arrival. I have half a dozen
letters for him, which I know not whether to
forward, so keep. But I do trust he will still
come.

Truly yours,

Nath[l] Hawthorne.

Liverpool, June 27th, 1854.

Dear Ticknor,

The affair of the confiscated box has turned
out better than I expected. Judicious meas-
ures having been used on my part, the Custom
House people have given it up, on payment of
duties. I say nothing of what was paid on the
cigars, (that being my own affair); but for
Fields' silver articles I paid £2, 4s. Nothing
was demanded for the books. I thank you
heartily for the cigars. They look first-rate, and
no doubt will prove so, when I try them — which
I have not yet been able to do, on account
of the hooping-cough. I have put the silver
things into my safe, and shall keep them there

for the present, in expectation of Fields' arrival by the next steamer.

If the bearer of despatches had done his duty, the box might have been delivered at once, without trouble or expense; but he went away, leaving it in the hands of the officers. His name is *Longbottom;* — and his bottom deserves to be kicked, be it long or short.

We are getting through the hooping-cough pretty comfortably; but it will be a long while before the children are in rugged health again. When they are well enough, I mean to take them into the country for a week or two, for change of air.

Truly yours,

Nath¹ Hawthorne.

Liverpool, July 7th, 1854.

Dear Ticknor,

I was even more disappointed than before, at Fields' non-arrival by the last steamer. He *must* come. If he can't, you must.

Mr. Beck writes me that he is going to Paris, and cannot therefore personally attend to the delivery of the silver articles &c., according to Fields' instructions. He has, however, given directions to Trübner & Co., how to dispose of them, and desires me to send them to their address. I shall hold on to them until after the arrival of one more steamer, in hopes of seeing Fields; — after which, if he don't come, I shall do as Mr. Beck suggests.

The hooping-cough is on the decline; and I intend, in the course of a week or so, to take my family into Wales or somewhere else, for change of air. If I could but have one week of my Concord hillside, it would do us more good than all the English air that ever was breathed. But it will be many a long day yet, before we see the old house again — perhaps never; for you seem to be in such a confounded mess there, that it quite sickens me to think of coming back. I find it impossible to read American newspapers (of whatever political party) without being ashamed of my country. No wonder, then, if Englishmen hate and despise us, taking their ideas of us and our institutions from such sources.

Truly yours,

Nath¹ Hawthorne.

P. S. One year yesterday since we sailed from America.

Liverpool, July 20th, 1854.

Dear Ticknor,

I am very sorry to find that we are not to see Fields, this year. Enclosed are some letters that have been on hand for him this long while. Does he expect immunity from sea-sickness next year? Or are we to have a railway across? He had much better have come now; but since it is not to be so, I wish *you* might find it necessary to come over and make purchases for the holidays. I see Americans enough, Heaven knows—but nobody that I care about seeing.

I have to-day deposited one hundred & fifteen pounds (£115) to your account with the Barings. This goes into the first year's pile; — my accession to office dating from the first of August. As matters now look, I shall not find the second year so profitable; but (unless they limit me to a salary) the office will still be worth keeping.

I have made a short, but very pleasant tour in North Wales, since I wrote last, and have also visited the Isle of Man, which is the most interesting place I have yet seen. Sophia and the children are now staying there; and I shall go to see them, to-morrow (Friday) and remain till Monday. The health of my family (and, indeed, my own) required a change of air, and nothing could be purer than the atmosphere of the Isle of Man.

You talk of intolerably hot weather. Until within a week past, we have had constant fires, both at house and office — and hardly comfortable at that. It is fine weather now, however — quite warm enough for comfort, and not a bit too warm for exercise; and if English weather were all like this, England would really be an earthly paradise. Unluckily, there is not more than a week of such weather in the whole year.

I think I have come to an understanding with the Custom House people; so that they will not meddle with any moderate-sized and honest-looking parcel — such as those you have been in the habit of sending me. The bearer of despatches should consider it his duty to see them through; and then there never would be any difficulty.

I have sent Fields' gimcracks to the care of Trübner & Co., together with Mrs. Howe's books. Mr. Beck wrote me that he had instructed Trübner what disposition to make of them. But I am out of patience with Fields for not coming. I returned from the Isle of Man sooner than I otherwise should, in the hope of meeting him here.

Good bye,

Yours truly,

Nath¹ Hawthorne.

Liverpool, Aug. 3d, 1854.

Dear Ticknor,

Enclosed are two letters for Fields, which ought to have been sent by the last steamer. If all his friends are as much disappointed at not seeing him, as I am, there must have been a sad time of it.

I send a small draft, given me by a young man, whom I supplied in funds and sent home by the last Cunard steamer. I think he will turn out an honorable fellow — otherwise I am in for his passage-money, which I guaranteed.

Mrs. Hawthorne and the children have returned, after spending a very pleasant fortnight at the Isle of Man. The hooping-cough has not quite disappeared yet, although they are much better.

It is impossible to say, as yet, what will be the effect of Guthrie's order, as regards Invoice-certificates, or my receipts. There are at present few or no transhipments of goods from our ports to the British provinces; all shipments being direct from here to Quebec &c. It is in the cold season, when their navigation is shut up, that they import goods through the States. I shall lose a good deal, but shall still be able to live — if nothing worse happens.

> Good bye,
>
> Nath¹ Hawthorne.

Liverpool, August 18th, 1854.

Dear Ticknor,

I enclose a package for Mr. Simon Brown, of Concord; he is editor of an agricultural paper (the name of which I forget) in Boston; and the package had better be sent to the office of the paper, than to his residence in Concord.

I sent Fields' silver things to London some time ago, and considered that I had done with them; but, a day or two since, I received back a silver shovel and pie-knife, for which no claimants could be found. Finding them thus providentially returned, I was a good deal inclined to confiscate them for the use and ornament of the consular table; but have finally concluded to send them to Mrs. Bennoch and Mrs. Craig, for whom Fields writes me they were intended. I don't know the locality of the latter lady, but will endeavor to find out.

I observe that a bill for the remodelling of the Diplomatic and Consular service was reported in Congress, August 3d, and referred to Committee of the Whole. I should suppose they can hardly have acted on it, in the brief remnant of the session; but if so, it cannot fail to have been most disastrous to my official interests. However, I am so sick and weary of this office, that I should hardly regret it if they were to abolish it altogether. What with brutal shipmasters, drunken sailors, vagrant Yankees, mad people, sick people, and dead people (for just now I have to attend to the removal of the bones of a man who has been dead these twenty years) it is full of damnable annoyances. If I could but make up those twenty thousand dollars, I should look very philosophically at whatever might happen next. After all, there are worse lives than that of an author—at least, when he is so fortunate in his publishers as I am. I suppose some persons would console themselves with the dignity of the office, the public and private dinners, and the excellent opportunity of playing the great man on a small scale; but this is to me a greater bore than all the rest; so that you see I have nothing to comfort myself with but the emoluments.

The hooping-cough is pretty well over; and we are all as well as could be expected.

Are you going to have a great crash among the commercial people? I hope I don't own any rail-road stock.

Truly yours,

N. H.

Liverpool, Aug. 25th, '54.

Dear Ticknor,

I send you three bills on the Secretary of State, amounting to $518.34; and one on B. Galbraith for $18.79 — which please to collect.

There is nothing new here. We are all in pretty tolerable health.

Truly yours,

Nath¹ Hawthorne.

Liverpool, Sept. 2d, 1854.

Dear Ticknor,

Enclosed are three second bills of exchange
on the Secretary of State. The three first
(together with one on B. Galbraith) went to
New York by the Cunard steamer of last
week.

We are having fine weather just now; and
I mean to take my wife and children into the
country, in the course of the present month.

Truly yours,

Nath¹ Hawthorne.

Liverpool, Sept. 15th, 1854.

Dear Tick,

There was no letter from you, last steamer,
so I suppose you were enjoying yourself at the
White Mountains, or elsewhere. Sophia and
the children have been at Rhyl for a week or
two. I have already paid them one visit; and
am going again to-day. Business is terribly
dull; and I hardly make enough to live on.

I wrote to Fields, last week, about a copy of

Parson's Poems, which Miss Mitford is very anxious to get, before she dies. Do attend to it.

I have drawn two bills on you ($25 each) in favor of E. P. Peabody.

In a hurry,

Yours ever,

Nath¹ Hawthorne.

Liverpool, Sept. 30th, '54.

Dear Tick—

I have not much to say, at present, except that business is very dull, and that you need not look for such remittances as I was in the habit of making, last year. I shall thank my stars if I do not have to draw on you.

Mr. Monckton Milnes wants me to send him half a dozen good American books, which he has never read or heard of before. For the honor of my country, I should like to do it, but can think of only three which would be likely to come under his description — viz. "Walden," "Passion Flowers," and "Up-

Country Letters." Possibly, Mrs. Mowatt's Autobiography might make a fourth; and Thoreau's former volume a fifth. You understand that these books must not be merely good, but must be original, with American characteristics, and not generally known in England. If you, or Fields, or anybody else, can produce any such, pray send them along. At any rate, send those I have mentioned; for my credit is pledged to supply the number Mr. Milnes asked for.

Whittier's book is poor stuff. I like the man, but have no high opinion either of his poetry or prose.

Send Lowell's "Bigelow Papers." He is very little known in England, and I take that to be the best thing he has written.

Truly yours,

Nath¹ Hawthorne.

Liverpool, Oct. 12th, '54.

Dear Ticknor,

I learn from the Cunard Agents that a draft on Captain Bell, U. S. N., by Mr. Rogers, endorsed by me, some three months ago, has not yet been paid, on account of their not having been able to find Captain Bell — he having left his former lodgings in New York. You can find out his present whereabouts on application to the Navy Department; or perhaps Bridge can inform you. I think there can be no doubt of Mr. Rogers being an honest and honorable fellow. He came to me on his return from St. Petersburg (where he had been to volunteer in the Russian service) destitute of funds, and without the means of getting to America. I supplied him with money and became security for his passage. He said that Captain Bell was in possession of funds belonging to him. If these facts are represented to Captain Bell, there can be no question that he will pay the draft, which is still in the hands of the agent of the Cunard line in New York. At all events, he will give you the address of Mr. Rogers, in Kentucky or Tennessee — I forget which. If he turns out to be a rogue, I will give up all pretence to being a judge of human nature. The draft was for £20.

What awful intelligence this is about the loss of the Collins steamer!

You speak of another book from me. There is no prospect of that, so long as I continue in office; but if the consular bill should pass at the next session, I shall soon be an author again. It proposes to allow no more than $7500 for the salary and all expenses of the office. No consul can live as a gentleman in English society, and carry on the official business, on those terms. But it would not cost me many pangs to resign. I hardly think, however, that the bill can pass during the short session.

Thank you for the two volumes of the Mosses. My books will now almost fill a shelf; and I hope to lengthen the list a little, yet.

        Truly yours,
                Nath¹ Hawthorne.

Liverpool, Oct. 26th, '54.

Dear Ticknor,

I will send the cheese in due season.

It will give me great pleasure to take charge of books and small packages, whenever you may have occasion to send them. There is no expense on them here (that is, when they go to London,) as I send them to the care of our despatch agent along with the Government-despatches. I have such an understanding with the Custom House officers that they will not again meddle with any package of the ordinary bulk.

Business continues very dull. I shall be glad when I have done with this office.

Your friend,

Nath¹ Hawthorne.

P. S.   I enclose a note from Mr. Cleaveland of Brooklyn, N. Y., in reference to my portrait for a publication of his. The idea of my paying for a new engraving of myself is altogether too good; but if you think fit to allow him the use of the old one, you may debit me to what amount you think fit. Not that I really care

anything about Bowdoin College, or Mr. Cleaveland, or his book; and I had as lief you would
refuse him as not.

However, I have told him that I would ask
you.

                                    N. H.

Do not put postage-stamps on any letters
which I send without them.

                        Liverpool, Dec. 15th, '54.

Dear Ticknor,

Per last Cunard steamer, I advised you that
I should have to draw for about £300, the
first of January.

I also asked you to pay to the Cunard-agent
(in New York, I presume) a draft of £30, for
which I made myself responsible on behalf of
Capt. Gibson. His name, by the way, is
Walter M. not I. W., as I miscalled him in my
last.

Mrs. Hawthorne sent you a cheese.

All the foregoing items you are no doubt
acquainted with already. There is nothing new.

Mrs. Hawthorne is not very well, and is a good deal depressed on account of the low state of her father, who, I think, will hardly survive the winter; and the very next arrival may bring us news of his decease.

If you learn anything about the probability of the passage of the consular bill, I should like to be informed of it.

It would gratify me to hear some particulars about Fields, and his matrimonial affairs. Are they coming out in the spring? I saw in a newspaper that Fields had lately published a volume of poems for private circulation among his friends. I don't want to press my friendship on any man; but I really thought I was one of them — one of the b-hoys — and ought to have received the poems.

Truly yours,

Nath¹ Hawthorne.

P. S. I hope Fields' silver pie-knife has reached Mrs. Craig before this time. I wrote to De Quincey about the mode of transmitting it, but received no answer, till at last a letter came from Miss De Quincey in Ireland. It

seems the old gentleman has shut himself up
in Edinburgh to follow his literary avocations
(and eat opium, I suppose) and all the letters
that go to Lasswade are sent first to his daughters in Ireland, and thence transmitted to him,
unopened. Miss De Quincey conjectured from
the seal and post-mark that the letter might be
from me, and so wrote to inquire the contents.
A book, which you sent for him, still remains
on hand; for his daughters hint that he opens
no letters or packages, in his present mood.

N. H.

Liverpool, Dec. 18th, '54.

Dear Ticknor,

I have inquired of the Barings about your
package of engraved plates, and am glad to
find that a parcel from Bogue, answering to the
description, was sent by the Pacific, three weeks
ago. I hope you will have received them in
time for use. Two cases of books from Trübner were sent by the America; and one case,
accidentally left behind, is to go by the Asia.

Is it possible that our friend John L. Clarke is dead? I see it noticed in the Boston Post of the 4th, but can hardly believe it. He had a secret affair which he meant to confide to me on his return to England; but I suppose he has taken it along with him to the "Silent Land." People seem to die now-a-days with less preparation and ceremony than they did in times past. I am truly sorry for this event.

Mrs. Hawthorne and the children are pretty well. Una has been boarding in town for the convenience of taking lessons in music, French, and dancing, but will come back to Rock Ferry at Christmas. We kept the New England Thanksgiving, as descendants of the old Puritans should; and we shall likewise keep Christmas, as everybody in England does.

Remember me to all friends.

Truly yours,

Nathl Hawthorne.

U. S. Consulate,

Liverpool, Jany 6th, '55.

Dear Ticknor,

I shall not have to draw on you before next steamer (to Boston,) and my draft, I hope, will not be nearly so heavy as at first anticipated.

Business continues dull; but I suppose it will revive a little, as the season advances. It remains to be seen whether its revival will be of any advantage to me. If Congress cut down my emoluments, the less business, the better.

Please to take special care of the three letters marked "B"; as they are from Mr. Buchanan, who seems to feel particular interest in their being safely transmitted.

Will you send me a copy of the Wonder Book and of Tanglewood Tales?

I long to see you — or anybody else from the old "Corner." Is Fields coming over this Spring?

Truly yours,

N. H.

Liverpool, Jany 19th, '55.

Dear Ticknor,

I am sorry to have given a false alarm; but as it turns out, I shall have no occasion to draw on you at present—having a good portion of the requisite amount on hand, and supplying the rest by drafts on the State Department for advances made. I shall lose nothing by this investment; and as to your advice not to lend any more money, I acknowledge it to be good, and shall follow it so far as I can and ought. But when the friend of half my lifetime asks me to assist him, and when I have perfect confidence in his honor, what is to be done? Shall I prove myself to be one of those persons who have every quality desirable in friendship, except that they invariably fail you at the pinch? I don't think I can do that; but, luckily, I have fewer friends than most men, and there are not a great many who can claim anything of me on that score. As regards such cases as those of Rogers and Gibson, my official position makes it necessary that I should sometimes risk money in that way; but I can assure you I exercise a great deal of discretion in the responsibilities which I assume. I have not been a year and a half in this office, without learning to say "No" as peremptorily as most men.

I enclose a letter to Rogers, which you will please to send to his direction, unless he has already deposited funds for your draft and that of Mr. Cunard. I also transmit the latter, which has been returned by Cunard, and paid by me. If Mr. Rogers neglects to refund, he is the meanest scoundrel that ever pretended to be a gentleman; for without my interference and assistance, he could have had no resource but starvation, or possibly a Liverpool workhouse. If he refuses to pay, himself, the fact of my aiding him, and of his extreme necessity at the time, should be stated to his brother or nearest relative, who, in the merest decency, cannot but pay the amount. But I still believe that he has a sense of honor in him.

It seems to be a general opinion that the consular bill will not pass. If it should, I shall (according to your statement) be at least a good deal better off than when I took the office. Reckoning O'Sullivan's three thousand dollars, I shall have bagged about $15,000; and I shall estimate the Concord place and my copyrights together at $5000 more; — so that you see I have the twenty thousand, after all! I shall spend a year on the Continent, and then decide whether to go back to the Wayside, or to stay abroad and write books. But I had rather hold this office two years longer; for I have not seen half enough of England, and there is the germ of a new Romance in my mind, which will be all the better for ripening slowly. Besides, America is now wholly given over to a d——d mob of scribbling women, and I should have no chance of success while the public taste is occupied with their trash — and should be ashamed of myself if I did succeed. What is the mystery of these innumerable editions of the Lamplighter, and other books neither better nor worse? — worse they could not be, and better they need not be, when they sell by the 100,000.

A gentleman here wishes for the Unitarian newspaper (the Enquirer I think it is called) published by Mr. Bellows in New York. You can subscribe for it in my name, pay in advance, and send the numbers in your regular package.

The children are delighted with the books you sent them.

I meant to write to Fields by this steamer, but fear I shall not have time. Please to convey to him my thanks for his slice of cake, and warmest congratulations on his marriage.

Your friend,

Nath[l] Hawthorne.

Liverpool, Febry 2d, 1855.

Dear Ticknor,

The apples have come to hand in fine order; and we thank you for them most sincerely.

The package of newspapers and letters was detained at the Custom House, a day or two. This happens whenever a new officer takes charge of the steamer; but all difficulties might be obviated if Mr. Glyn (the Despatch Agent) would be kind enough to put the official seal and label on the parcel. The package need not even have my name on it, nor be in any way distinguished from those that are to be transmitted to the Minister; for I shall be sure to recognize it. In accordance with orders from the State Department, I am entitled to receive my own private letters &c. by the same conveyance with the despatches; and the above is the only method by which their prompt delivery can be secured. The Custom House authorities always give them up, but only after I have been put to the inconvenience of making application, and proving my right to them. Will you see to this?

I told you in my last that I should not be under the necessity of drawing on you. It gives me much pleasure to see that my affairs are in such good condition, and I feel truly obliged to you for your kind care. I hardly venture to hope that I shall do so well, this present year; but anyhow, with the assistance of my pen, I shall manage to live, even if my office should cease to be worth holding. I wish I could make a book calculated for schools. Can't you think of any?

In my last, I recollect, I bestowed some vituperation on female authors. I have since been reading "Ruth Hall"; and I must say I enjoyed it a good deal. The woman writes as if the devil was in her; and that is the only condition under which a woman ever writes anything worth reading. Generally women write like emasculated men, and are only to be distinguished from male authors by greater feebleness and folly; but when they throw off the restraints of decency, and come before the public stark naked, as it were — then their books are sure to possess character and value. Can you tell me anything about this Fanny Fern? If you meet her, I wish you would let her know how much I admire her.

I don't think of anything more to say, just now.

Truly yours,

Nath¹ Hawthorne.

Liverpool, Feb. 16th, 1855.

Dear Ticknor,

I send you back the bill of exchange — the drawer (or at least, the signer) not being in good credit with the Barings; so that I thought it best not to present it for payment. I don't want this money here; and if E. P. Peabody has really paid it over to you, please to add the sum to my balance. It was money which I paid on her behalf here in England, and I did not look to have it refunded, but am perfectly willing, since she chooses to do so.

Business never was so dull between England and America as it has been this winter. I make out to live, and a very little more, but am not growing rich.

We are all pretty well. I am going to dine with the mayor at the Town Hall, and expect to make a foolish speech to-night, and wake up with a headache tomorrow morning. Luckily, the speeches at the mayor's dinners are never reported. It is very difficult for an American to speak in public in a manner to suit both

countries, just at this time, when there is a
good deal of hostile feeling towards England,
on your side of the water, and not a little on
the part of England towards us. I shall be
true to my country, and get along with John
Bull as well as I can. The time will come,
sooner or later, when the old fellow will look
to us for his salvation. He is in more danger
from his own allies than we are either from
him or them.

Truly, in haste, yours,

Nathl Hawthorne.

P. S. Did you notify Capt. Gibson that you
paid Cunard the amount of his draft? I wonder
whether his intended father-in-law is a rich man.

Liverpool, March 2d, 1855.

Dear Ticknor,

I have made up my mind to the worst, on
the subject of the consular bill. It is hardly
possible that the Senate should oppose it, after

its passage with such a rush through the House. I shall be better able to determine on my future course, after becoming acquainted with the details of the bill. If I find that I can hold the office without a positive expense to myself, I think I shall remain here for one year longer, for the sake of seeing more of England — then go to Italy for perhaps another year — and then home. After all, I shall probably find reason to think that everything has been arranged for the best; and I shall at least come home in better worldly condition than I went away. If I really cannot pay the expenses of the office and live out of the salary, I shall go to Italy immediately, and perhaps come home in the autumn. The mere idea of this gives me a little touch of home-sickness. I do love old Massachusetts, in spite of its ten thousand varieties of nonsense.

I enclose a letter to be mailed for California; but not knowing how much the postage will be, I must request you to pay it on my behalf.

We are all very well. Will Fields bring his wife out here this season? I wish he would.

Either he or you must come; or I shall never get acquainted with our friends in London.

Truly yours,

Nath¹ Hawthorne.

Will you see if the letter to E. P. Peabody is rightly directed? I have not her direction at hand.

Liverpool, March 30th, 1855.

Dear Ticknor,

I see by one of the papers you send me that an amendment was appended to one of the appropriation bills, providing that the Diplomatic & Consular Bill shall not go into operation till after the 1st of January next. Bridge has seen the President, who confirms the above. This will give me nine profitable months from the present time; — after which it will be time enough to decide what to do next. If I can keep my present clerks, I should not mind holding on till, say, October of next year, or possibly till the next administration comes in.

But if, next January, I find the money coming in very fast, it will be best for me to decline a new appointment, and keep hold of what emoluments I can get before my successor appears. This would allow me a clear run of pretty nearly or quite a year from this time; and though it will not be so good a year as the first one, it will add very considerably to the weight of my balance-sheet. The affair turns out so much better than I at first expected, that I feel as if a piece of good luck had happened to me. Pecuniary troubles do not affect me long, nor very severely; and, according to all appearances, I shall get a pile big enough to live on, even putting my pen out of the question. As for luxuries, you must print and sell enough of my future scribblings to supply a reasonable share.

I am going to live as moderately as I can, during the rest of my stay here, consistently with comfort, and the desirable object of seeing whatever is most interesting in England. I shall give up my house as soon as possible, and go into lodgings. This will abridge the number of servants, and make it impossible for me to entertain people—which is very expensive here. Beggars, too, and tourists without funds, will not find their way into my pocket so easily as heretofore. After all retrenchments, I shall still have to spend a good deal of money; but, by strict economy, I think I could manage so as to leave a margin of the $7500. If I expected to continue long in office, I should use my endeavors to get a separate consulate established at Manchester — whereby this office would be immensely relieved. But I would not on any account turn off either of my clerks; and therefore I shall leave my successor to find out the methods of diminishing the clerical labor of the office.

We are all well, and in excellent spirits. It is our intention, this summer, to spend some time at the lakes, and to visit Scotland, and do up various other sight-seeing; and, as we shall not have a house on our hands, this can be done with the less inconvenience and expense.

Truly yours,

Nath Hawthorne.

Liverpool, April 18th, 1855.

Dear Ticknor,

This is a first-rate Mail Bag; and will be very serviceable to me, together with its fellow, after I leave the office.

Business is getting brisker than for some time past; and I shall soon be able to renew my remittances. Indeed, you would be safe in drawing on the Barings for £200, now, although I have not yet positively deposited it. No doubt, I shall advise you of having done so, by next steamer.

I don't think I am quite so well contented here, as before this disturbance about the Consular Bill. My mind has been unsettled by the thoughts of going away, and I do not easily reconcile myself to a longer period of drudgery, after expecting a release within a few months. Ten thousand dollars will pay well enough for a year's servitude; but I doubt whether I could be induced to stay here for any less consideration.

We expect to give up our house on the first of June; and shall then go into the country, and shall make several removes and expeditions during the summer. I have confined myself too closely to the consulate during my stay here. There is no sense in making a prisoner of myself, and so I mean to enjoy England while I have an opportunity.

I wish you would come over — or Fields — or Whipple — or somebody that I care about. America begins to be dim in my remembrance; and my exile is not yet half over; for we shall spend at least two years on the Continent before returning.

Truly yours,

Nath¹ Hawthorne.

P. S.   Please to pay carriage on the package for Salem, which I enclose, and charge to me.

Liverpool, April 26th, '55.

Dear Ticknor,

I send O'Sullivan's deed, and wish you would ascertain whether it lacks anything to make it valid. He would like, if possible, to have the sale kept secret for the present, because it was his wife's property, and he hopes to redeem it; but, I should think, it might be recorded without interfering with this object. The agent of the property is Francis R. Tillou, ex-Recorder of New York. Nothing need be said to him, as he will continue to pay the rent to O'Sullivan, who will account to me. There is no fear of another conveyance, nor, I suppose, of an attachment, it having been his wife's property. From what Bridge tells me (and he has it directly from Pierce) my official position will remain as heretofore, until after the first of January. In that case, it would not be advisable for me to accept a re-appointment, which will then be made; because I should have to account to the Department for the whole receipts of the preceding six months, which will no doubt amount to thousands more than my salary — and on which, unless I make a return, the Government can establish no hold. This seems to be the President's and Secretary's understanding of the case. I must say, I should be very unwilling to remain here another year, unless the advantages were to be very decided.

One thing at present perplexes me. Without further advices from the State Department, I shall not know whether to levy the fees on the old or new system. The latter, it appears to me, will give a much larger aggregate than the former, and so far, would be for my advantage; but then, if I comply with one part of the law, must I not comply with the whole? Then, again, I doubt whether, after the present quarter, the Department will honor my drafts for advances made to seamen, &c.; and, if these drafts are refused, the whole support and maintenance of such seamen will come out of my own pocket. It will still be a profitable concern, to be sure; but you see what a d——d bother is likely to arise from this uncertain state of things. I consider it best, however, to let matters take their course, and not to hazard bringing on a peremptory and unfavorable decision by applying to the State Department for instructions. The only part of my receipts for which my bonds could possibly be held responsible, would be the sums I receive from masters of vessels for wages of seamen left behind; and these always fall far short of the advances made by me for the support of seamen. Moreover, even those sums could not be ascertained by the Department, unless I choose to make a return. I have Uncle Sam on the hip, you see; — and good enough for him, the infernal old villain! If I could only make up my mind to be as much of a rogue as he is, I might remain in office and thrive by it.

I enclose some letters on which I have put no stamp, because I do not know how much the postage will be. The new law, I see, requires pre-payment within the limits of the States; but these are for a person in Canada. If it is necessary to prepay in these cases, please to do so, and charge it to me; — if not, mail them without payment.

I have deposited two hundred and seventy pounds (£270) with the Barings to your credit. It looks now as if I should nearly or quite make up the $20,000 (including my investments with O'Sullivan and Bridge) before July; and if the President adheres to his purpose of keeping the old system in force, the subsequent six months can hardly fail to give me five or six thousand more. If so, I shall be well enough satisfied.

I want you to send Howitt's "Adventures of a Boy in Australia," for Julian.

Please to tell Mr. Glyn that the Cunard agent and purser refuse to designate the bearer of Despatches in the list of passengers, on the ground that it is contrary to their rule. It seems to be a very foolish rule; but that makes no difference to an Englishman. Perhaps Glyn can persuade the Purser to do it. His bundle of papers, this week, is so long that it will not go into my bag. Whenever possible, it shall be put in, even to the exclusion of my own packages. Tell him so.

I thank you for Mrs. Mowatt's plays. They are silly enough to be pleasant reading.

Good bye,

Nath¹ Hawthorne.

Liverpool, May 11th, 1855.

Dear Ticknor,

I thank you for Kingsley's book, which I think a first-rate one; also, on Julian's behalf, for the Australian adventures, which has just met his wishes.

In my last, I advised you of a deposit with the Barings of £270. I shall probably soon send you drafts to a considerable amount on the State Department. Business is getting brisker.

I want you to send me a copy of the Liturgy of King's Chapel, published by you. The New York Inquirer has not been sent for some weeks. Do you receive it?

I wish you would take a convenient opportunity to go to Concord, with Fields or Whipple, or some other friend — dine at the Middlesex Hotel, or anywhere else where you can get good feed and liquor — and take a look at my place, and charge the expenses of the trip to me. First, read over the lease which I gave Mr. Bull, (a copy is in your keeping,) and then see whether he is complying with the terms of

it, as respects the improvements to be made
on the land in front of the house. It will be a
great injury to me if he does not promptly ful-
fil the conditions as to setting out an orchard
&c.; and I have some reason to think that he
has not, thus far, quite come up to the contract. Do not give yourself any extra trouble
about this matter; but, when you want a pleas-
ure-excursion, I should be glad to have you
make it in that direction; — and remember me
over the champagne, if there is any longer such
a liquor in old Massachusetts.

I enclose a note drawn by Mr. W. E. Tyler,
in favor of Una and Julian, to whom this
money was given in their infancy, by a friend.
Dr. Peabody invested it in this way; but perhaps it had better be in your hands, to be
re-invested. This I must leave to your judgment.

This is the worst pen I ever wrote with.

> Truly yours,
>> Nath¹ Hawthorne.

I am nearly out of postage-stamps. Please
to send some more.   N. H.

Liverpool, May 27th, 1855.

Dear Ticknor,

I have little or nothing to say to you just now. Business goes on tolerably well, and I hope soon to advise you of another remittance.

We intend to set out on our rambles about England, soon after the first of June. I shall spend much of the summer away from Liverpool, but shall pay frequent visits to my consulate; and I rather think matters will go on about as well as if I were constantly on hand. At all events, I have a right to some recreation — for I have had very little hitherto.

It is a very disagreeable office; but some amusing incidents happen occasionally; — for instance, I send home by this steamer a Doctor of Divinity who has been out here on a spree, and who was brought to my office, destitute, after a week's residence in a brothel! I wish you could have heard the lecture I gave him. He shook in his shoes, I can tell you. Not knowing whether I should ever have another opportunity of preaching to a Doctor of Divinity (an orthodox man, too) I laid it on without mercy; and he promised never to forget it. I don't think he ever will. You will probably see his name in the list of passengers,—but don't breathe a word about it.

Truly yours,

Nath[l] Hawthorne.

I want some more postage-stamps, but they will be of no use to me if Mr. Glyn declines to be the medium of conveying my letters. Our Government grows more intolerable every day. I wish it might be changed to a monarchy.

Liverpool, June 7th, 1855.

Dear Ticknor,

Everything goes on pretty well with us. We hope to take our departure for the country in the course of next week; and I mean to enjoy the summer, and let business take care of it-self—or, rather, let Mr. Pearce and Mr. Wilding take care of it, which they are far better able to do than I. I shall be within reach of tele-graphic notices, and can always make my appearance at the consulate within a few hours.

I paid off the Government-bills, yesterday, and shall draw on the State Department, in your favor, for something like three hundred pounds, by the next steamer or the succeeding one. Before quitting town, I shall deposit any spare cash I may have on hand, to your credit with the Barings—to the amount, perhaps, of £150. You see, I am approaching pretty closely towards the $20,000; and I shall have still another set of bills to draw on Government, next month, for my expenditures during the present quarter. The amount of these, together with whatever may accrue during the month, will not fall much short of my *minimum*, which I have always set at $20,000; and the next six or seven months, I hope, will do considerably more. But I shall be glad when I have done making money; for it is too apt to draw a man's thoughts from better things.

You promised Una to send her a new photograph of you, in case we would return the one you left here, which the children complain of as looking fierce and ill-tempered. I decline giving up this one, until I have an opportunity of comparing it with the one you propose to send; for this is a perfect likeness, and I take great pleasure in looking at it; — and I see nothing more disagreeable in its expression than a kind proposal to take something to drink.

Truly yours,

Nath¹ Hawthorne.

P. S.   I think I have already asked you for some more postage stamps.   Please to put stamps on all the letters which I mark *paid*, and charge to my account.

N. H.

P. S. 2d   If you know George Curtis' (the Howadji's) address in New York, please to put it on the letter to him.

Leamington, June 21st, 1855.

Dear Ticknor,

We left Rock Ferry for this place on Monday, and arrived same evening in good order.

It is a beautiful place, and unlike all other English towns (so far as I have seen them) looks perfectly clean. We have taken an entire house (except what is occupied by the mistress of it) at 13, Lansdowne Crescent, and shall be most happy to receive a visit from you, any time within a month. I doubt whether Sophia will go back to Liverpool again, except for a visit, now and then. According to my calculation, we shall be able to live more cheaply at watering-places and country-towns, or even in London, in respectable lodgings, than we have heretofore done in Liverpool, or than we could at Mrs. Blodgett's boarding-house. Our whole expenditure here, with these ample accommodations, will not exceed seven guineas a week. We are beginning to get an insight into English economical customs. They know how to be comfortable and make a good appearance, on a great deal less than Americans spend for a poorer result.

I shall go back to the consulate whenever business may require my presence, but mean to spend the greater part of the time with my family.

Mr. Wilding will send you, by this steamer, bills on the Department for $1399.92. I deposited £125 to your credit with the Barings, on Friday last.

I send a letter for Mary Ahern, which I wish you would direct to her at Eastport. I got her a place as stewardess on board the ship John Knox, which sailed for that place, last week; and I believe she has engaged with the captain to continue in office during the year.

Massachusetts must be a very uncomfortable place, just now, with your liquor laws and other nonsense. I wish we could annex this island to the Union, and that I could have an estate here in Warwickshire. We mean to go to Stratford on Avon tomorrow, and there are a great many other desirable places within easy reach.

Truly yours,

Nath¹ Hawthorne.

Lowwood Hotel,
Lake Windemere, July 18th, '55.

Dear Ticknor,

We came from Leamington to the lakes in the beginning of last week. I don't know where we shall go next — perhaps to London — perhaps to Scotland. It is well I did not set out on my travels sooner; for I doubt whether I could ever have contented myself to spend a fortnight together at the consulate.

Mrs. Hawthorne's health and strength seem to improve, and I feel more encouraged about her than when I wrote last. She shall never reside in Liverpool again, for any length of time, whether I keep the office or resign it.

I have seen none of the American newspapers by the last steamer. Well — I am sick of America, and feel it a relief to escape all knowledge of its affairs, for a week or two; for I have been more bothered with my own countrymen and their troublesome peculiarities, since coming to England, than ever before in my life. I shall need a residence of two or three years on the Continent, to give me a sense of freedom.

Truly yours,

Nath¹ Hawthorne.

Liverpool, August 1st, 1855.

Dear Ticknor,

Since my last, if I mistake not (but I forget what was the date of my last) I have been to the lakes, and have been enjoying myself a good deal. Mrs. Hawthorne's health seems to have improved. She is now at the Rock Ferry Hotel; but we shall take a new trip before long. It will not take me a great while to get a thorough acquaintance (as thorough as a foreigner can ever get) with England; for, by living among them, and living as they do, I have come to understand them differently from what Americans usually can. I think my Journals (which are getting to be voluminous) would already enable me to give you a book that would compare well enough with Grace's

" Haps & Mishaps." But I don't mean to publish any such book.

I shall probably soon send you some more bills on Government — the last of the kind you are ever likely to receive from me. Business is not very brisk now-a-days; but that does not concern me so much, since the new act has come into operation. For my part, I should not care if the Liverpool trade were to dwindle down to absolutely nothing — leaving only the notarial business. I wish nobody any harm; but failures, shipwrecks, and all sorts of commercial disaster, would have a direct tendency to fill my pockets; — whereas, a prosperous state of trade only gives me the more unpaid business to perform. So you see, I am somewhat in the situation of Doctors and undertakers, who thrive by the misfortunes of their fellow-creatures. But success to Uncle Sam, say I, in spite of all the mischief the old rogue has done me.

Truly yours,

Nath[l] Hawthorne.

Liverpool, Aug. 17th, '55.

Dear Ticknor,

There is nothing new since my last. We are still staying at the Rock Ferry Hotel. Mrs. Hawthorne has been taking cod-liver oil, and seems to be in a more promising state; but I hardly think it will be safe to trust her in England during the ensuing winter. I have not yet heard from Bridge or the President in reference to my leave of absence. If not given, it will certainly be taken, whenever necessary.

I send some copies of Allingham's poems; and I wish you would have them distributed to people tinctured with poetry and such non-sense — to editors of magazines or newspapers — and to anybody who will take the trouble to notice them. Will not Fields give them a puff in the Transcript? — it used to be his organ in my literary days. Do ask Whipple to take them into his gracious consideration. There is great merit in some of the pieces. "Cross-Examination," for instance, is wonderfully pithy. I can't say I have read them all, for I dislike poetry. But I know the author, and should be

glad to have him get an American reputation —
which he deserves as much as a good many
writers whose works you have published. I
enclose a list of persons to whom Allingham
has already sent the poems. Please to write
"With the Author's compliments,"— on the
title pages of those you distribute.

Nothing else at present. My bills on Government (which will probably be ready for next
steamer) will amount, I think, to nearly £400
— to be added to my pile.

Did I advise you of £125 deposited with
the Barings two months ago or more?

N. H.

Liverpool, August 31st, 1855.

Dear Ticknor,

Mrs. Hawthorne's health seems to have improved considerably; but she agrees with me
that it is best to change the air before cold
weather comes on;—so she, Una, and Rosebud, are going to Lisbon, where the O'Sullivans
are anxious to receive them. Julian will re-

main in England with me. They will sail from
Southampton, probably, towards the end of
September; and we shall spend most of the
intervening time either in London or the north
of England. We expect to start for London
next Tuesday. Very probably, I shall pay her
a short visit before she returns from Lisbon.

I send three bills of exchange, to the aggregate amount, I think, of $2206.37 — which will
be quite an important addition to my small
accumulations. Don't you think I have property enough, now, to resign upon? I want to
do so most damnably, but will try to hold on
another year, unless the coming Congress makes
the office worse than it looks now. I should not
wonder if it did.

A gentleman of Liverpool wishes me to inquire if any of the Boston papers would like a
correspondent here. He is a business man, of
great intelligence, and of liberal and indepen-
dent views in politics; he could give reliable
information as to the actual state of the markets,
and fair conjectures as to what it is likely to
be. He was employed, last year, on the Wash-

ington Globe, and gave good satisfaction. I don't know exactly what his price is; but, I guess about $5 per letter, of a newspaper column — which is ridiculously low. Would you be kind enough to make a few inquiries among the editors? He is not a penny-a-liner, but a man in business.

Read, and then seal, the letter to Owen H. Peck.

I feel a little homesick, now and then, but not to any great extent; and it is well for me that I don't, for it will be three years yet before I darken the doors of the old corner-store. I have gained a better acquaintance with my own countrymen, since taking this office, than in all my previous life; and, to say the truth, I wish to get farther off, in the hope of liking them better. Two years on the Continent will perhaps revive my patriotism.

I made a convert to total abstinence, yesterday. It was a sea-captain, who has fallen into dissipated habits; and I preached to him with such good effect that he asked me to draw up a pledge, which he signed on the spot, and declared that he felt himself a new man. On the strength of this good deed, I thought myself entitled to drink an extra glass or two of wine in the evening, and so have got a little bit of a headache. " Physician, heal thyself"!

Remember me to all friends. Tell Colonel Miller that I met Miss Cushman, a little while ago, at Windermere, and expect soon to see her in London.

Truly yours,

Nath¹ Hawthorne.

Liverpool, October 12th, 1855.

Dear Ticknor,

I returned hither from Southampton, last Tuesday, having shipped Mrs. Hawthorne and two of the children for Lisbon, on board of the steamer Madrid. We parted in pretty good spirits; and the physicians say there is no question but a few months on the Continent will remove her complaints. It is very likely I shall pay her a visit during the winter. Julian remains with me; and we have established ourselves at Mrs. Blodgett's — where I feel quite at home, especially in the smoking-room.

I have spent the last month almost entirely in London, and know it pretty well now; for I was never weary of rambling about, and peeping into all the odd holes and corners I could find. The last day I was there, I called on Trübner, and found him so good a fellow that I was sorry not to have called sooner. I did not seek society; but I saw by chance one or two people that interested me, and who seemed glad to see me — among others, Leigh Hunt, whom I like very much, partly, perhaps, because he is half an American. I wish you could do him some of the good offices which you do for other English authors, by republishing his works. It is strange that he has not a greater popularity on our side of the water, since he possesses many of the literary characteristics which we are quickest to recognize.

Bennett told me that there is an illustrated edition of the Scarlet Letter in preparation, in the style of Evangeline, with engravings by

Vizitelly. In fact, he told me this as much as a year ago, but the matter was to be kept secret, nor does he yet know who is to publish it. He has seen some of the illustrations, and thought them good. I don't know when it is to come out.

I shall not be content to hold on here in expectation of $30,000. A smaller sum must answer the purpose; and I have little doubt that Congress will make such changes for the worse in the law, that I shall find it advisable to resign. The sooner the better;—money cannot pay me for the irksomeness of this office, at least, only a very large amount can do it; and I really think I should be glad to have Congress put the question of my remaining here at rest, by breaking down the office altogether. This very morning, I have been bored to death by a woman; and every day I am beset with complainants who I wish were all at the devil together. But I can get along well enough with men, if the women would only let me alone.

I want you to send me a copy of the House

of the Seven Gables, bound in dark calf, in antique style.

I had a letter from a German the other day, proposing to me to pay him for making a translation of my entire works, taking the chance of selling the copyright to the German booksellers!! I rather think the Germans are the meanest devils in the world; though the English deserve a pretty prominent place in that particular. After all the slander against Americans, there is no people worthy even to take the second place behind us, for liberality of idea and practice. The more I see of the rest of the world, the better I think of my own country (not that I like it very enthusiastically, either;) and, thank God, England's day is past forever. I have such a conviction of the decline and fall of England, that I am about as well satisfied as if it had already taken place. And yet I like John Bull, too.

Truly yours,

Nath[l] Hawthorne.

Liverpool, Oct. 26th, 1855.

Dear Ticknor,

I have this morning received Mrs. Hawthorne's first letter since her arrival in Lisbon. She and Rose suffered terribly from sea-sickness on the voyage, owing to the swell in the Bay of Biscay; but Rose was quite well before landing, and my wife was a great deal better. Her cough was already much alleviated, although the rainy season was not quite over. Una was not sea-sick at all; but she says she wanted you to walk the deck with her, during the voyage. I feel confident that they will all derive great benefit from the change of climate.

As for myself, I am living quietly at Mrs. Blodgett's, among the sea-captains and transient American tourists; and our talk is so very unlike what I hear among my English acquaintances, that I could almost fancy myself back in America again. There is a strange idea, on this side of the water, that we are going to send a filibustering expedition against Ireland!! If we have any design of the kind, I go in for attacking England at once; and there is very little (in the way of fortifications) to hinder an American fleet from sailing up the Mersey. I should like well to be superseded in my consular duties by the arrival of a Yankee Commodore or General. The truth is, I love England so much that I want to annex it, and it is by no means beyond the scope of possibility that we may do so, though hardly in my time.

According to the last quarter's accounts, I am to pay over to Government, nearly £800, which, if that damnable law had not gone into effect, I should have transmitted to you. This is sheer robbery. I am disgusted with the business, and can hardly bear to think of continuing at the present miserably reduced rate of compensation. I *must* and *will* resign, next spring, at farthest. I wish that you (in a quiet way, so that it cannot possibly be known) would cause inquiries to be made into that New York property, which I bought of O'Sullivan. It was a part of the estate of his wife's father. You can easily ascertain, I presume, (and without giving rise to any scandal) whether there was any legal impediment, through Dr. Rodgers's will, or otherwise, to the sale of the property by O'Sullivan and his wife; for I have so little confidence in O'Sullivan's business qualifications (though entire confidence in his honor) that I have sometimes suspected that this might be the case. Do have the affair managed very cautiously. There was one portion of the property which O'Sullivan had purchased after Dr. Rodgers's death, in order to prevent its going out of the family.

I wish for the above information, because the safety, or insecurity, of that property will of course influence me, as regards my continuance in office. If it is safe, I can afford to resign.

Truly yours,

Nath¹ Hawthorne.

Liverpool, Nov. 9th, 1855.

Dear Ticknor,

We have all been in commotion here, for a fortnight past, in expectation of a war; but the peaceful tenor of the last accounts from America have gone far towards quieting us. No man would be justified in wishing for war; but I trust America will not bate an inch of honor for the sake of avoiding it; and if it does come, we have the fate of England in our hands. If the Yankees were half so patriotic, at home, as we on this side of the water, I rather think we should be in for it. I HATE England; though I love some Englishmen, and like them generally, in fact.

I had letters from Mrs. Hawthorne a few days since. Her health was improving, though she had not yet got rid of her cough, the weather having been rainy, with intervals of warm sunshine. She is delightfully situated with the O'Sullivans, and sees kings, princes, dukes and ambassadors, as familiarly as I do Liverpool merchants. Nevertheless, she is homesick; and I believe we should all be glad to return to the old house at the Wayside tomorrow. But I fear we shall have outgrown that house before we get back, and I shall at least be compelled to make more additions to it, if not to build a new one. I sometimes doubt whether this European residence will be good for us, in the long run. All of us will come back with altered habits, accustomed to many things which we shall not find at home; and as for the children, (though they imagine that they love America above all the rest of the world) they will really belong on this side of the water, rather than on that. And if my wife's health shall prove to have been radically impaired here (which however I will not anticipate) it would throw an awful balance on the wrong side of the account. These are gloomy thoughts, growing out of my solitary bachelor-state, I suppose.

I have as yet received no copy of Hiawatha from Longfellow or yourself; but Bogue has sent me the English edition, and I like it very much. It seems to me perfectly original — the annexation of a new dominion to our poetical territories; and he seems to have caught the measure and rhythm from the sound of the wind among the forest-boughs. I believe it is not yet published here. As to its success, compared with his other writings; that must be matter of experiment, and I should deem it rather a doubtful one. But, at any rate, it puts my estimate of his originality a peg higher; and I love to see him still on the ascent.

I have requested Mr. Deane, the bearer of despatches, to deliver into your care a shawl, which was left at our house some months ago by Miss Martha Cochran, a friend of Mrs. Hawthorne's. I think, (but am not certain) that she resides in Springfield, and I believe Mr. Skinner of Boston married her sister. Will you have the shawl disposed of so that it may reach her? Mr. Deane is a connection of Horace Mann's, and seems to be a sensible and agreeable, but rather raw specimen of the Western Yankee. He has been traveling on the Continent with his wife, a niece of Horace Mann's.

I shall wait with much interest for the response of Young America to the hostile demonstrations on the part of England. If I mistake not, John Bull is now heartily afraid of the consequences of what he has done, and will gladly

seize any decent method of getting out of the
scrape. If we do not fight him now, I doubt
whether he will ever give us another chance.
He has partly learned what he himself is, and
begins to have some idea of what we are.
There has been a great change, on both these
points, since I first came to England.

Truly yours,

Nathl Hawthorne.

Liverpool, Nov. 23d, 1855.

Dear Ticknor,

There is nothing new here since my last.
We are awaiting the arrival of the New York
steamer with a good deal of interest, not doubt-
ing that it will bring a response to the warlike
demonstrations of this Government. I cannot
conceive that there is really any chance of a
war. The English people will not let their
Government go to war with us; not from any
liking for America, but from a wholesome apprehension of the consequences. This feeling
is very manifest, all over the country.

I had letters from Mrs. Hawthorne in the

early part of this week. She writes in better
spirits than heretofore, and tells me her cough
is improving under the influence of warmth and
sunshine. She happened to arrive before the
rainy season was over, and therefore found the
atmosphere about as moist as that of England.
There will now be fine weather until February,
when, if necessary, I shall go to Lisbon, and
take her up the Mediterranean. It is strange
that I receive no answer to a request for a con-
ditional leave of absence, which I made to the
President several weeks ago. I wish you would
enquire of Bridge whether he knows anything
about this. In one point of view, it would be
better for me to resign, than to take a long
leave of absence, for, in the latter case, the law
not only allows me no salary, but requires me
to support the consulate at my own private expense. Congress (if it has any common sense
at all) must see the absurdity and injustice of
this, and amend the law; but meanwhile I remain in a quandary. No words can express
how I long to consign the consulate to the
Devil, or to any other successor whom the

President may appoint. But I am not yet tired of England, and should like to spend another summer in travelling over it; and it will be much more convenient to do it with a salary than without.

I asked you, some time since, to send me a copy of the "Seven Gables," bound in calf. It has not yet come to hand.

After Parliament meets, I intend to go to London again, and see a little more of society than at my last visit. I think I never should be weary of London, and it will cost me many pangs to quit it finally, without a prospect of returning. It is singular, that I feel more at home and familiar there than even in Boston, or in old Salem itself. Being the great metropolis of the world, it is every man's home.

I find the only consolation of my bachelor-life in the cigar-box. I dine out rather oftener than while I lived on the Cheshire side; but this is a great bore, and I should be glad to escape it altogether.

Truly yours,

Nath¹ Hawthorne.

P. S. I enclose two letters for Col. Lawrence, which be so kind as to send to his house immediately.

Liverpool, Dec. 21st, 1855.

Dear Ticknor,

I want you to pay the drafts of John Dike, of Salem, to the extent of $100, (one hundred dollars) for the benefit of W. Manning, an old and poor relation of mine.

There is nothing new here. We are having terribly cold weather; and I think I never suffered so much from it in America; — our houses being much better calculated for winter than English ones. It is impossible to keep warm by the fireside.

I received letters this morning from Mrs. Hawthorne, and she still reports a progressive improvement of her health.

You came through the Hiawatha business better than I anticipated. I am glad to find that public opinion will not support an Editor in unjustly deteriorating a book, more than any other piece of goods.

Julian is well and hearty.

With best regards to all friends,

Truly yours,

Nath¹ Hawthorne.

P. S. Our bag was unlocked, this last time, when I received it. Was this accidental? — or did the Despatch-agent send it so on purpose? Pray reason him out of any such nonsense, if he does it for official reasons.

N. H.

One of the enclosed letters is for Horace Mann's family. I have forgotten what town Antioch College is in. Please to direct it properly.

Liverpool, Jany 17th, 1856.

Dear Ticknor,

I don't understand this botheration about the bag. Col. Lawrence wrote me that Secretary Marcy allowed him to receive packages from this country through the medium of the Despatch Bearers, and that the Despatch agent at Boston had promised him to deliver them, when forwarded in my bag. Did Glen ever make any such agreement?—and if so, why did not he stand to it? Tell Glen this, and let him ask an explanation of Col. Lawrence. Meanwhile, the Assistant-Secretary of State has written to me, laying blame at my door. The Devil take him, and Glen, and Lawrence, and the Government, and everybody connected with it! I can justify myself (and shall do so) by quoting a letter of instructions from Buchanan, while Secretary of State, to one of my predecessors—instructions which have never been revoked, and which have been acted on, up to this time. I shall continue to send the bag, although hereafter I shall certainly decline having anything to do with Col. Lawrence's parcels. I shall be glad if you will let him know the difficulty into which he has brought me.

I have had no letter from Mrs. Hawthorne, I believe, since my last to you.

Julian thanks you very much for the two books. I have read part of Mrs. Ritchie's work, and am much interested in it. I wish I was acquainted with her. It gives me pleasure to hear of the great success of Hiawatha. On this side of the water, too, it is received with greater favor, I think, than any of Longfellow's former works, and has gained him admirers among some who have hitherto stood aloof. Nevertheless, the following lines have been sent to me—

> "Hiawatha! Hiawatha!
> "Sweet Trochaic milk and water!
> "Milk and water Mississippi
> "Flowing o'er a bed of sugar!
> "Through three hundred Ticknor pages,
> "With a murmur and a ripple,
> "Flowing, flowing, ever flowing—
> "Damn the river!—damn the poet!"

Everybody seems to be seized with an irresistible impulse to write verses in this new measure. I have received a lampoon on myself (in manuscript) of as much as a hundred Hiawatha lines, some of them very laughable. I would send you a copy, but have already transmitted the verses to Mrs. Hawthorne.

I still hear nothing from the President about my leave of absence; and if it were granted, I could not very well make use of it. My official responsibilities are much heavier than under the old law,— for instance, I have many thousand dollars of public money (which should have been my own) now in my keeping; and I must remain at my post, either to take care of it or to pay it over. I cannot express, nor can you conceive, the irksomeness of my position, and how I long to get free from it. I have no pleasure in anything — a cigar excepted. Even liquor does not enliven me; so I very seldom drink any, except at some of these stupid English dinners. I have got to dine with the mayor shortly,— for the last time, I fervently hope; for my soul is in peril already with the lies I have told at the mayor's dinner-table, in regard to the good feeling of America towards England.

Truly yours,

Nath¹ Hawthorne.

END OF VOLUME I.

*LETTERS OF HAWTHORNE TO
WILLIAM D. TICKNOR*

LETTERS OF

HAWTHORNE

TO WILLIAM D. TICKNOR

1851 – 1864

VOLUME II

NEWARK   NEW JERSEY

THE CARTERET BOOK CLUB

1910

Concord, April 30th 63

Dear Ticknor,

I thank you for that
excellent lot of cigars, and
expect to have, as much enjoyment as a man can ra-
tionally ~~expect~~ hope for in this troublesome world, while smoking
them after breakfast and
dinner. Their fragrance
would be much improved if
you ~~would~~ come and smoke
in company. Yours truly
Nath' Hawthorne

LETTERS OF HAWTHORNE TO
WILLIAM D. TICKNOR

Liverpool, Feb. 16th, 1856.

Dear Ticknor,

I have had a call, this morning, from Mr. Holbrook of Boston: — the same who was shipwrecked, some time ago. Being rather short of funds, I have supplied him with £5, (five pounds) which he will hand to you on his arrival in Boston. He intended to have crossed in this steamer, but was disappointed of a berth. He is a queer old fellow, and appears to have Robinson Crusoe's mania for travelling. He tells me that he is going to get you to publish his autobiography; and, so far as I can judge by his oral narration, it will be an interesting and profitable work. His last adventures have been in the East, and he was present at the Siege of Sebastopol, and almost had his head knocked off by a cannon-ball. He will probably return home by the steamer Glasgow, which is to sail from Glasgow a week from today.

There is nothing new here. Which one of you is coming over, this season?—and how soon do you start?

Truly yours,

Nath¹ Hawthorne.

Please to pay (and charge to me) the carriage of the parcel for my sister.

Liverpool, Feby 27th, 1856.

Dear Ticknor,

I send you three small drafts for amounts due me on account of protests. One of them should have been forwarded upwards of a month ago, but was forgotten.

Glen has evidently interposed me as a shield between himself and the censure that was justly due for some neglect of his own. I have no key to the Government-despatch-bags. They are never opened at this office, and are sent forward precisely as received here. The newspapers &c. for Glen, which are put into my private bag, were never put under lock and key until we began to run this bag. It is quite impossible that any of the Government-despatches should have been delayed by my sending Colonel Lawrence's parcels. However, it is of no consequence — but I know what to think of Mr. Glen henceforth.

Mr. Holbrook did not go by the Glasgow steamer, as he intended, but will sail by the steamer that brings you this. I send his memorandum for six pounds which I have advanced him.

I have not yet heard of Mrs. Hawthorne's arrival in Madeira; there having as yet been no steamer from thence.

My health and spirits are considerably better than in the earlier part of the winter. I begin to eat and drink again. About the twentieth of March, I mean to pay a visit to London, and shall probably remain there twenty days — ten in the first quarter of the year, and ten in the second; so that Uncle Sam will not be able to grab my salary on plea of over-absence. There is a pleasure in getting around such a mean old scoundrel as Uncle Sam.

28*th*. I have just received letters from Sophia
& Una at Madeira. They were terribly sea-sick
on the passage, and found the weather cold
and rainy on their arrival; but Mrs. H. speaks
very hopefully about her health.

March 1*st*. There is no news. The war-
talk has entirely died away; and I hope, on
the American side of the water, we shall say
nothing more about fighting, unless we really
mean to come to the scratch. It is considered
very doubtful here whether the conferences at
Paris will result in peace with Russia; and this
is probably one of the reasons why the English
tone is less hostile with regard to us.

Tell me in your next how soon you or Fields
intend to be in England. One of you must
come, of course.

I have been reading Grace Greenwood's
book, and like it pretty well. I shall write to
her soon.

Mr. Holbrook has just called in. He will
bring you the latest accounts of me.

Truly yours,

Nath[l] Hawthorne.

Liverpool, March 15th, 1856.

Dear Ticknor,

The books are beautifully bound; and I have a greater respect for my own works than ever before — seeing them so finely dressed. I should like to give them to Mrs. Hawthorne, rather than the King of Portugal.

Mr. Dallas arrived two days ago. He seems to be a respectable old gentleman; but I should not take him to be a very able diplomatist, and he certainly has a difficult business to handle. Buchanan is worth ten of him; and even he has made no great hand of it. Mr. D. is well provided as respects the female part of his establishment — *seven* ladies, I believe, to all of whom I had to be civil! I thank Heaven I am not keeping house, and that there was no hospitality to be exercised.

I intend to go up to London next Thursday, and spend two or three weeks, including the last ten days of March, and the ten first days of April. By thus dividing my term of absence between two quarters of the year, I shall defeat Uncle Sam's shabby efforts to filch away my

salary. During my stay in London, I will see
your friends there, and some of my own, and
hope to have an agreeable time. This has been
a dreary winter, but I find myself in better
health and spirits, now that it is over. But we
still have wretchedly cold weather.

I had letters from Mrs. Hawthorne, the first
of the week. The weather in Madeira had
been worse than ever before was known, with
violent rain and wind; and there being no possibility of fireside comfort, in that part of the
world, she had not been quite so well as in
Lisbon. Latterly, however, there had been a
few genial days, and she immediately began to
improve. I feel it hardly safe for her to return
to England even to spend the summer, which,
you know, is just as damp and almost as cold
as the winter. If she *does* return, I do not
mean to let her come so far north as Liverpool.
She might spend a few months pleasantly in the
south of England, and in London; and in October, or thereabouts, we would finally go to the
Continent. I have had about enough of England—that is to say, I feel as if I understood

something of English life and character, and nothing remains but to make excursions to various points. This I can do in the course of the summer.

There is no news here.

Remember me to all my friends, and believe me

Sincerely yours,

N. H.

Liverpool, April 11th, 1856.

Dear Ticknor,

I staid in London exactly three weeks, and returned only last night, after having enjoyed myself gloriously — owing principally to Bennoch's kindness. I lived rather fast, to be sure; but that was not amiss, after such a slow winter. My health and spirits are much better than when I went away.

I have not your letter by me, but am much pleased with the satisfactory summary you give of my affairs. If it becomes necessary to give up the consulate, before another winter, I shall

do so without much apprehension as to my
pecuniary prospects, though perhaps I may
spend a little more than my income in travelling and residence abroad. But I think I can
write a book or two that will set it all right. I
need not say how much I feel indebted to you
for your kind and careful stewardship of my
affairs. I think all the better of mankind (and
especially of publishers) for your sake.

Bridge's note must be renewed, if he wishes it.

Fields writes me that, in case of a war between
America and England, he is going to fight for
the latter. I hope he will live to be tarred and
feathered, and that I may live to pour the first
ladleful of tar on the top of his head, and to
clap the first handful of feathers on the same
spot. He is a traitor, and his English friends
know it; for they all speak of him as one of
themselves.

I heard from several people in London a
strong and confident assurance that Longfellow
is coming over, this summer. Are there any
grounds for this report? If he cares about
being lionized, let him come *now;* for his

reputation can never be higher nor better. I wish he would come.

I enclose a letter for Washington Irving, whose present address I do not know. Please to direct and send it.

I wish you would send me two copies of Thoreau's books — "Life in the Woods," and the other one, for I wish to give them to two persons here.

Mrs. Hawthorne has had very rainy weather in Madeira; and there being no fireside comforts to be had, her health had suffered somewhat, in consequence. Rosebud, too, had been quite ill, but was convalescent at the last dates. I regret that they did not stay in Lisbon.

I can think of nothing else to say at present. Mr. Holbrook's account shall be settled, and the receipted bill sent by next opportunity.

   Truly yours,

     Nath¹ Hawthorne.

P. S. I saw (among about a thousand other noticeable people) your author, Charles Reade — a tall, stoutish, fair-haired, light-complexioned man, thirty years old, or upwards. He did not make a very strong impression on me. I like his books better than himself; not that I saw any fault in him either. I tell you this because you particularly wished me to see him.

I want you to send me a cheap edition of James's novel, the "Old Dominion."

Liverpool, April 24th, '56.

Dear Ticknor,

On examining into the state of my accounts with the Department, I find that I shall be safe in letting you draw on me for £350 (three hundred and fifty pounds,) immediately. I keep my funds and those of the Government in the Borough Bank of Liverpool; and the amount is getting so heavy that I think it best to withdraw as much of it as I can. I shall no doubt be ready to pay your draft on presentation; but as I might possibly be away from Liverpool at the moment, you had best draw at three days sight.

I shall likewise send you, either by this steamer or the next, bills on the department for about £150; so that, altogether, you will have $2500 to invest for me. If I could remain in the consulate till the four years are quite expired, I should not fall very far short of $30,000; but there is very little prospect of my holding on through next winter. Unless Mrs. Hawthorne's health shall be more improved than I venture to hope, I shall quit England for the Continent in November next. It would be convenient to pile up a little more money; but I thank Heaven for what I have, and, at all events, shall have no great fear of starving.

I am much disappointed to learn that there is little prospect of seeing either you or Fields here, this summer. It will be a long time yet before I shake hands with you, on your side of the water. To say the truth, the longer I stay away, the less I feel inclined to come back; and if it were not for my children, I question whether I should ever see America again. Not but what I love my country; but I can live more to my individual satisfaction elsewhere. I am happy to say that Julian does not share my feelings at all. He got a black eye, the other day, fighting with some English boys, who, he says, abused his country; but I believe the quarrel began with his telling them that it was his highest ambition to kill an Englishman! He is a sturdy little devil, and as strong as most boys two or three years older than himself.

I observe, in one of the late numbers of the Little Pilgrim, a description of Grace's baby. I wonder she did not think it necessary to have a committee of her subscribers present, when she was brought to bed!

I thank you for the poem — "The Angel in the House" — which you sent me by last steamer. I thought it very good — always excepting the measure, which has somewhat of the lame-dromedary movement which poets now-a-days seem so partial to.

I forget whether I told you of my spending two or three days in the Camp at Aldershott, and messing with the officers of a regiment there. I fraternized very strongly with them all, from the Colonel downwards; and I don't think there will be any war between England and America.

>Truly yours,
>
>Nath¹ Hawthorne.

I enclose a letter for Mrs. Maders, O'Sullivan's sister. I do not know her address in New York; and you had better direct it to the care of somebody there who knows the family.

>Liverpool, May 10th, '56.

Dear Ticknor,

In my last, I told you to draw on me for £350, at three days sight, and likewise enclosed bills for about £100 more.

I have received letters from Mrs. Hawthorne, by which she tells me that she will probably arrive in England about June 14th. There has been some warm weather, and her health has improved very rapidly; but I am afraid she is coming back too soon. However, an English fireside, in some one of the southern counties, will probably be as good a climate as she can find.

Since I last wrote you, I have made a trip to Scotland, visiting Glasgow, the Highlands, Edinburgh, and whatever else was interesting. It was very cold; but there being no rain, I saw the country to good advantage, although I meditate a longer visit hereafter.

I see that the American papers publish a report of what I said at the Lord Mayor's dinner —a vile report, too, obliterating all my points, and exaggerating the nonsense of the thing. I was about half-seas over when I got up to speak; but I swear I spoke a devilish sight better than that. Ask Bennoch if I did not.

My health has grown vastly better since I began to move about, and I mean to get away from the consulate as often as possible, during the summer.

In a hurry,

Your friend,

Nath. Hawthorne.

Liverpool, May 23d, 1856.

Dear Ticknor,

I have good accounts from Mrs. Hawthorne, and expect her back in little more than three weeks from this time.

I went to Manchester yesterday, and dined with Bennoch and some friends of his. He is very well, and talks much of you and Fields. I wish you could have been with us, last night, either or both of you; but (judging by my own case) I think it would have cost you a little bit of a headache. Bennoch is coming to Liverpool pretty soon, to dine with me. Won't you be of the party?

I think I told you, in my last, of my having been to Scotland. I keep a journal of all my travels and adventures, and I could easily make up a couple of nice volumes for you; but, unluckily, they would be much too good and true to bear publication. It would bring a terrible hornet's nest about my ears.

There is nothing new.

Your friend,

N. H.

Liverpool, June 6th, 1856.

Dear Ticknor,

The bag with the newspapers was delivered as usual; and I think you had better send the letters as heretofore — saying nothing to Glen about the matter. I shall send mine by way of Washington, unless circumstances should require an immediate delivery, in which case they can go by post.

I myself procured the abolition of the bearers of despatches; for, by their carelessness, they had several times caused me to be blamed; so I wrote a long despatch to the Department, setting forth the objections to the system, and advising that the despatches be confided to the Pursers of the steamers. I wish I had included Glen and the other despatch-agents in my attack.

Your draft for £350 in favor of Barings has been presented and paid, without waiting for the ten days sight.

Our relations with England seem to me to bear a more pacific aspect than for many months past. Frank Pierce never did a better thing than in recognizing Walker's Government; it has brought John Bull to his bearings, and, with his customary growling and grumbling, he is going to back out. Crampton ought to have been dismissed more promptly; but it is better late than never. Most people here think that Dallas will be sent home, and, I believe, he is himself very uneasy. I hope he *will* be sent home, because it will be such a very foolish act on the part of the British Government—and, moreover, he will be no loss to anybody.— But I am of opinion that they will let him stay.

In ten days more, I hope to see Mrs. Hawthorne, and, for that purpose, shall go to Southampton. We shall spend, I think, a good part of the summer in the southern part of England. Bennoch is going to Germany with his wife in July, and he has most kindly offered us his house at Blackheath, during his absence. It will depend on Mrs. Hawthorne, whether we avail ourselves of his kindness. We will, on one condition; — that you will come over and be our guest, during the two months that we should keep the house. Why not?

       Your friend,

           Nath¹ Hawthorne.

         Liverpool, June 20th, 1856.

Dear Ticknor,

Bridge has written to me about the note, telling me that it was his impression that the loan was for *three* years. I thought so too; and was surprised when you told me that the time of payment was approaching. At any rate, let him have the money as long as he wants it, even should it be till the day of doom.

Mrs. Hawthorne arrived at Southampton ten or twelve days ago, in good health and spirits, only a little tired with her voyages and travels. She has little or no cough left, and earnestly wishes to spend another winter in England. We shall decide about this, after trying the effect of the climate upon her. For the present, she is staying near Southampton; but we shall take Bennoch's house early in July. Are not you coming over to pay us a visit? If you will, Mrs. Hawthorne shall read you my journal, containing a full and particular account of my visit to London — which would be worth a mint of money to you and me, if I could let you publish it.

I saw Bennoch yesterday, on my way hither from Southampton. He is in good condition.

Pray do not be so hopeless about our political concerns. We shall grow and flourish, in spite of the devil. Affairs do not look so very bad, at this distance, whatever they may seem to you who are in the midst of the confusion. For my part, I keep a stedfast faith in the destinies of my own country, and will not be staggered, whatever happens.

You see, I was right in my opinion that Dallas would not be sent home. We have gained a great triumph over England, and I begin to like her better now; for, I can assure you, Englishmen feel that they have given up forever the pretensions to superiority, and the haughty tone, which they have hitherto held towards us. We have gone through a crisis, and come out right side up. Give Frank Pierce credit for this, at least; for it was his spirit that did it.

As regards the New York property, I never bought it with any view to profit, and am quite content if it is good security for the sum advanced upon it. If this be the case, we will let the matter rest as it is.

Thank you for the two De Quincey books.

Truly yours,

Nath¹ Hawthorne.

Liverpool, July 17th, 1856.

Dear Ticknor,

I have been in the South of England and in London for nearly three weeks past, and have now established Mrs. Hawthorne and the children at Blackheath. They are delightfully situated, and if I could only spend my whole time there, I should ask nothing better for the next two months. I got into a new vein of society, on this last visit to London, and have seen a good many interesting people. It is much pleasanter than stagnating in this wretched hole; but I must come back hither, now and then, for the sake of appearances.

After we leave Blackheath (if Mrs. Hawthorne's health continues good enough to allow of her staying in England) I think of taking a house or lodgings in Chester, for what further time we may spend here. It is an interesting old town, and the air there is much better than in Liverpool, and I could attend to all my official duties without inconvenience. It is not quite certain, as yet, that I shall not resign in the autumn; but, if possible, I am inclined to stay the four years out.

By next steamer, I shall probably send you bills on Government, amounting to somewhat more than £200.

I saw your namesake, Mr. Ticknor, in London, at a breakfast. I heartily wish it had been yourself.

I shall return to Blackheath in the course of next week.

With remembrances to all friends, most sincerely yours,

Nathl Hawthorne.

P. S.   A little draft (for $10) will be presented to you in favor of J. D. Howard, a poor devil who was in the Salem Custom House with me.

[From Mrs. Hawthorne.]

My dear Mr. Ticknor,

We have been the objects of perfectly magnificent hospitality to a gentleman of Oxford — former mayor of Oxford, now alderman — a gentleman of the kindest heart — most liberal hand — sagacious, sensible — & of indefatigable activity.   We wish to make a delicate return in the way of memorial, & I have suggested to Mr. Hawthorne a set of his own works — *very splendidly* bound — Wonder book & all — Will you order this to be done as soon as possible — to send by the next steamer, if that is not too soon ?   This gentleman has abundance of innocent vanity & self appreciation, & would be pleased at such a gift from N. Hawthorne, Author of Scarlet letter—&c—!!!! Mr. Hawthorne was asked at Stanton Harcourt whether he was the author of " *The Red Letter A ?* "

Was not that funny?

In greatest haste with very kindest regards, dear Mr. Ticknor — I am

truly yours,

S. Hawthorne.

Sept. 7th, 1856.

Blackheath Park.

P. S.   We leave Blackheath in a few days for the North —

Mr. Hawthorne has been reading my note and put all those exclamations on the other side —

and he says I must say to you that haste to send the volumes must not in the least impair the perfection of their binding — also that it would please the gentleman to have his name in gilt old English letter

R. J. Spiers, Esq:

somewhere on the outside.   Now I have told

you his name, pray burn my note, because I have said he was vain. * * * * But we like and respect him very much.

[Hawthorne has added these lines at the end of Mrs. Hawthorne's letter:]

To

R. J. SPIERS, ESQ.

in black-letter, on the side-cover.

N. H.

[This letter follows on the fourth page of the same sheet:]

Dear Ticknor,

If I were to send a set of my books to everybody who shows me kindness, it would exhaust an edition.   However, you may do as Mrs. Hawthorne says.   We had a very jolly time in Oxford.

I enclose ·a letter to E. P. Peabody, and I particularly wish that you will learn her present direction, and forward it without delay.   She has taken it into her head that Mrs. Hawthorne is extremely ill; and, unless prevented seasonably, I shall expect to see her on this side of the water. This would be exceedingly awkward and inconvenient; moreover, Mrs. Hawthorne is better, at this moment, than at any time since the first six months of her residence in England. Of course, the above paragraph is for yourself only. E. P. P. was at Dr. Wesselhoeft's, a short time since; at any rate, I suppose her brother will know her whereabouts.

I expect Mrs. H. from London, tomorrow, on her way to Southport — a sea-side residence where she will spend the rest of the autumn. Our winter campaign is not yet arranged.

The time I spent at Blackheath and its neighborhood was most delightful, and I shall be eternally obliged to Bennoch.

The new Bill makes no alteration of importance, as regards my consulate,— except that there may be a small allowance for office rent. Thank God, it will not be many months, at longest, before I am free.

Truly yours,

N. H.

Liverpool, Sept. 12th, '56.

Liverpool, Sept. 26th, '56.

Dear Ticknor,

I enclose bills on the Department to the amount (I think) of $1312.83. I forget what was the date of my last remittance; but I believe you have not yet advised me of the receipt. I begin to feel as if it were not worth while to grow much richer; but (Mrs. Hawthorne's health permitting) I shall hold on to the end of my term. The office (but this is a secret for yourself alone) is not worth less than $10,000, clear of expenses, in spite of the reduction.

You did not write by the last steamer. My budget of letters from America never seems complete, without a line from you.

We are now residing at Southport, a seashore place about 20 miles from Liverpool. The physicians have recommended the sea-air for Mrs. Hawthorne until December, or later; and I think we shall take a house for three months at Southport. Our vagrant life, for the last year or two, has brought me acquainted with a great variety of English scenes and modes of living. We shall know how to prize a home, if ever we get back to one; but, I must confess, I am in no great hurry to return to America. To say the truth, it looks like an infernally disagreeable country, from this side of the water.

Bennoch is coming to dine with me at the Adelphi Hotel, on Saturday week. I mean to have a party of ten or twelve, and should be most happy to see you among them. Can you come?

I hope you noted my request about a finely bound copy of my romances &c for Mr. Spiers.

Truly yours,

Nath¹ Hawthorne.

P. S. N. C. Peabody writes me that the house at Concord is in need of repair, to the amount of about 25 or 30 dollars— I have told him to employ a carpenter, and have the bill sent to you.

N. H.

Southport, Oct. 10th, '56.

Dear Ticknor,

I can't imagine what has become of you; for it is now two months, at least, since I had the pleasure of receiving one of your little notes. As for Fields, he never writes.

Bennoch dined with me at the Adelphi, last Saturday, and spent Sunday here at Southport with us. This is a dull and dreary little watering-place; but the air suits Mrs. Hawthorne, and we have taken a house for the next three months. I go into Liverpool (twenty-three miles), almost every day; but I am staying at home to take care of the children, to-day, while Mrs. Hawthorne goes to town to call on Mrs. Ward, who sails tomorrow. I must confess I sigh for London, and consider it time mis-spent to live anywhere else.

Bennoch is by this time on his way to Germany, to bring home his wife, who has received great benefit from her residence there.

We expect a governess to take charge of the children, next week; and then Mrs. Hawthorne and I will be able to go sight-seeing, as long as the season will permit. We are meditating an excursion to Yorkshire pretty soon. If we go to Paris, it will not be sooner than February, about which time the east-winds set in, all over

England. Mrs. Hawthorne looks and feels more like herself, since we came to Southport, than at any time since our residence in England.

The wise ones prophesy great commotions in France, and all over the Continent. Very likely there will not be a quiet spot to live in, just when we are ready to go thither. But there seems to be no stormier prospect any where, than in our own country; and I find myself less and less inclined to come back, with every budget of news that comes from thence. I sympathize with no party, but hate them all — free-soilers, pro-slavery men, and whatever else — all alike. In fact, I have no country, or only just enough of one to be ashamed of; and I can tell you, an American finds it difficult to hold up his head, on this side of the water, in these days. The English expect to see the republic crumble to pieces, and are chuckling over the anticipation. This is all nonsense, of course; but it grinds me, nevertheless.

I see Whipple has come out as a politician, on the Fremont side. It is a pity.

By last steamer (I think it was) I sent you bills on the Department to the amount of $1312.83; and you have not advised me of the receipt of a preceding batch, the date of which I do not precisely remember.

Truly yours,

Nath¹ Hawthorne.

P. S.   I enclose the Dinner-bill for your edification.

RADLEY'S
Adelphi Hotel
Ranelagh Place, LIVERPOOL.

NOTICE.   THE CHARGE FOR ALL THE SERVANTS IS INCLUDED IN THE BILL, (EXCEPT TO THOSE WHO STAY ONLY A FEW HOURS) VIZ. WAITER, CHAMBERMAID & PORTER, AND IT IS RESPECTFULLY INTIMATED THAT ANY FURTHER PAYMENT IS UNNECESSARY.

ALL INFORMATION OF STEAM BOATS, RAILWAYS, POST OFFICE & EVERY ENQUIRY OF IMPORTANCE TO BE MADE OF THE CLERK OF THE BAR.

Hawthorne, Esq.

Oct. 4   10 Dinners   Turtle
Haunch of Venison &c 15/   7 10
Sherry & Biscuits   7
1 B Punch   4 6
2 – Hock   1   1
1 – Sherry 6/   Ale 1/   7

4 – Champagne	2	
2 – Moselle Cup	1	1
Dessert & Grapes	1	5
Ice Creams & Cakes		15
Brandy 3/ Liqueurs 8/		11
1 Pine 27/6 Lights 10/6	1	18
1 B Port		12 6
3 – Claret	1	10
Teas and Coffees		10
Cigars 6/ Brandy 2/		8
1 B Madeira		9
Waiters		10 6
	£20	19 6
Brandy No. 55 1/ Rum 6/		7
5 Bfts & Ham 10/		10
Bedrooms		7 6
	£22	4 –
Servants attendance		6
Settled	£22	10 –

J. S. Kemp
for J. Radley

[On the verso of the bill is this list in Hawthorne's handwriting.]

Mr. Hawthorne

Mr. F. Bennoch	Mr. Joseph Pollock
Mr. C. Swain	Mr. Charles Holland
Mr. H. A. Bright	Mr. Albert Mott
Mr. Ely	Mr. Geo. Melly

Mr. Babcock

U. S. Consulate, Nov. 6th, '56.
Dear Ticknor,

The books are entirely satisfactory.

I want you to help me through a business, which, very likely, you will think me a fool for engaging in. Miss Bacon, some time ago, applied to me for assistance in getting her book on Shakespeare published. On reading the work, I found it to possess very great merit, though I don't at all believe in her theory as to the authorship of the plays; — however, as it was impossible to get it published otherwise, I have agreed with Parker & Son, of London, to publish it on my assuming the pecuniary responsibility and writing an introduction. Acting on Bennoch's advice, I shall put the book into Parker's hands, in print; and it is now being printed in London under Bennoch's supervision. 1000 copies will be printed; and of these I shall send you 500, with your name on the title page. You must excuse the liberty, as there is no time to consult you beforehand; and you may be assured that it is not a work which you will have any reason to be ashamed

of. Parker, I suppose, will sell the volume at
10/6 or 12/. You must put at such price as
will best suit our market. No doubt, I shall
lose something; but having tried to help this
poor woman, I do not like to desert her without doing my utmost.

The title is "The Shakspeare Problem; by
Delia Bacon." Advertise it if you like; and I
suppose you will receive the unbound sheets
early in December — perhaps sooner. By the
by, Miss Bacon herself does not know of my
pecuniary responsibility; — so say nothing of it
to anybody.

You sent me some months ago, the poem of
the "Betrothed." I liked it very much, and
want the "Espousals," which I see you have
now published.

No part of Miss Bacon's book has ever been
published. The article in Putnam's Magazine
does not make a portion of this work.

Perhaps you have not observed that the
new Consular Bill (to take effect next January)
authorizes the President to appoint "Consular
Pupils," who are to be distributed among the

various consulates, and will receive $1,000 per annum for their services. If your son Howard is at leisure for a few months, I should consider it a good opportunity for him — not, of course, as a permanent situation — but merely as a visit to England. I should require no duty whatever of him; for I shall keep all my own clerks as long as I remain in office. Howard might (so far as I am concerned) go where he liked, and do what he liked; and I think he might live, and see England pretty thoroughly, within the limits of his salary. The appointment, however, is not in my gift; but the President would probably have regard to my recommendation; and by next steamer I will send a letter for him, to be forwarded or not as you see fit.

It is a most foolish provision of the law, and will have no better purpose than to burthen the consulates with idle and dissipated lads, whom their friends at home are anxious to get rid of. If Howard comes, he will at least save me from one such incumbrance.

You speak of my chances under Buchanan.

Nothing earthly would induce me to stay in office another winter after the coming one.

Sincerely yours,

Nath¹ Hawthorne.

Liverpool, Nov. 21st, '56.

Dear Ticknor,

I enclose the letter to the President, which you can forward if you like.

In my last, I wrote you about the great affair of "The Shakspeare Problem." I doubt whether it gets through the press this month.

My wife is pretty well, and so are the children — colds excepted.

In a great hurry,

Yours truly,

Nath¹ Hawthorne.

Liverpool, Jany 2d, '57.

Dear Ticknor,

I wish you all the good wishes of the season, and I hope I shall see [you] (on this side of the water, however) before the end of the year. I take it ill of Pierce that he does not at once comply with my personal request about your son. He cannot have any objection to the step proposed; but it would be just like him to let the whole matter slip, from pure negligence. Can you think of no means of drawing his attention to the subject?

Julian, and Una, and Rose, have all received your kind presents of books, and are delighted with them.

I send you the title page of Miss Bacon's book, as transmitted to me by Bennoch.

The Shakspeare Problem
Solved by
Delia Bacon

With a preface by
Nathaniel Hawthorne,

Boston
Ticknor, Fields, & Co.
London.
J. Parker & Son, West-Strand.

I don't know how the printing gets on. Bennoch sent me about 150 pages, a week or two ago, and I have had nothing since. It will be an octavo volume of some 500 pages, I should judge. I am an utter disbeliever in Miss Bacon's theory, but am much impressed with the depth and acuteness of her criticism of Shakespeare. I think the book will sell, to a certain extent, in America, and will attract a good deal of notice from literary people on this side.

Mrs. Hawthorne has been very vigorous, but caught a cold, a few days since, which has put her back a little. Still, she has gained much, and is better now than at any time since crossing the Atlantic. I shall rejoice, on her account, when we get to the Continent. For my own part, on the whole, I should be well content to spend the remainder of my days in England, though certainly not in the office of Liverpool Consul. Of this last I am heartily sick, and would not keep it at $20,000 per annum. By the way, let me know what I have to live upon. I shall send you bills on the Department to a considerable amount, very soon; and there are four or five thousand pounds in bank here, some of which is mine, though the rascally Government will take far the largest share. Still, I must be within bounds in considering myself possessed of $5000 more than what is already in your hands. My expenses, however, have been large for the past year.

Your friend,

Nath¹ Hawthorne.

Liverpool, Jany 31st, '57.

Dear Ticknor,

Miss Bacon's book is printed, I believe, with the exception of my preface, which does not yet exist, but, I hope, will be written tomorrow. To say the truth, the book is d——d hard reading, but contains wonderfully good matter, nevertheless.

I have had all sorts of trouble in my consulate, lately;—indeed, I always do, but now more than ever. The Liverpool philanthropists are aroused about the enormities on board of our ships, and would like to have me run a-muck with them against the American shipmasters; and as I choose to take my own view of my own duty, they censure me pretty harshly.

They will hardly succeed in crowding me off my track; but it is not to be denied that there is nothing in this world so much like hell as the interior of an American ship. I have made repeated statements on this subject to our Government; and, long ago, I wrote most earnestly to Charles Sumner to bring it before Congress. Had he busied himself about this, instead of Abolitionism, he would have done good service to his country and have escaped Brooks's cudgel. I offered to supply him with any amount of horrible facts; but he never noticed my letter.

N. C. Peabody will present a small draft on you; and I want you to pay, when presented, a bill for a new pump at the Wayside. I wish I had a better house to live in, when I come home. It will be necessary to repair and enlarge it; and I sometimes think it would be well to sell the place, and look out for a more inhabitable one. If I once begin to build, I shall spend more than I can afford. What do you think of this matter? The fact is, I do not take root anywhere, and never shall, unless I could establish myself in some old manor-house like those I see in England.

I have written (some time ago) to Bridge to communicate to the President elect my purpose of resigning, in the course of a few months; and I should not wonder if my successor were already fixed upon. Poor Devil! I pity him, whoever he may be; especially as he will never get so much solid sweet out of the office as I have. I cannot express to you the pleasure with which I anticipate my release.

I presided, last night, at a meeting of American shipmasters, and made a speech! ! ! It is easy enough to speak, when a man is cornered and *corned;* but I here make a vow never to raise my voice so as to be heard by more than six people, nor to speak more than a hundred words together, after quitting this consulate.

Truly yours,

Nath¹ Hawthorne.

Liverpool, Feb. 13th, 1857.

Dear Ticknor,

Miss Bacon's book is all in type, and I have written and sent off my preface. The title is as · follows —

"THE SHAKSPERE PROBLEM SOLVED,
by DELIA BACON.

With a preface by Nathaniel Hawthorne,
Author of the Scarlet Letter &c

Boston,
TICKNOR AND FIELDS."

I should think it time to advertise; though I
don't know how soon your part of the edition
will be sent you. It makes an octavo volume
of between five and six hundred pages. Thank
Heaven, I have done with it—except paying
the printer &c.

Mrs. Hawthorne and all of us are pretty well,
and my spirits begin to rise with the certainty
that my official trials are within six months of
their termination. I have sent my resignation,
to take effect from August 31st. Buchanan
may choose to turn me out sooner; but I
should suppose he would prefer taking the
office on my own terms, as the old fellow and
I are very good friends. The office-holders, on
this side of the water, are very uneasy about
their prospects, and with good reason, I think.

Do — DO — DO come to England, this Summer. I shall take it much amiss if neither you nor Fields come. I expect to leave for the Continent in the course of September, and, meanwhile, shall visit such parts of Great Britain as I have not yet seen. In Italy, perhaps, I shall begin to be a literary man again; for I feel some symptoms already. It is a pity I can not take advantage of my residence in England to publish something while I remain here, and to secure the English copyright. But it is quite impossible.

Your friend,

Nath¹ Hawthorne.

P. S. I enclose a book, which was left here for you by William Channing. Rev. James Clarke will call and tell you about it.

Liverpool, Feb 26th, '57.

Dear Ticknor,

Miss Bacon and I, just at present, have come to a deadlock. She thinks my Preface (which is already in print) does less than justice to her book, and refuses to let the publication go forward, unless I make it more favorable. Having already gone to the limit of my conscience, I cannot comply with her wishes; and as Parker will not take the book without my preface, I do not quite see how the difficulty is to be settled. Bennoch is trying to arrange it, and I suppose the lady will have to come down in her pretensions. Nothing will satisfy her, short of my expressing full belief in the correctness of her views.

Since I last wrote, our house at Southport has been broken into, and robbed of various articles of plate, clothing &c. The thieves were put to flight by Julian, who was awakened by the noise, and frightened them away by calling to his mother. He takes to himself great credit for his valor on the occasion; but the truth is, neither he nor anybody else knew what had happened, till the next morning. This is the second time I have been robbed, since we came to England; the first time, they took all our silver forks and spoons, and these last robbers had to content themselves principally with electro-plate. The thieves have been discovered, and committed for trial.

I enclose a first of exchange for £30, for money advanced to Mr. Charles D. Tyng, and a draft for £10, for a subsequent loan.

I believe I have nothing else to say.

Your friend,

Nath¹ Hawthorne.

Liverpool, March 13th, '57.

Dear Ticknor,

Miss Bacon has accepted my preface, after cutting out a few paragraphs of not much importance. The last I heard of the matter, she and Bennoch were engaged in a discussion about the title of the book; but she is the most impracticable woman I ever had to do with— a crooked stick. No doubt, your copies will soon be forwarded, now.

I enclose C. D. Tyng's second of exchange for $151.57. By last Cunard steamer, I forwarded the First, and likewise a subsequent draft for $50.50.

I am well pleased with the condition of my finances, as shown in your statement; and if I were now at home, I should hardly think it worth my while to be any richer. During my voyages and travels, however, I shall have to spend a little more than my income; but will make it up by subsequent industry and economy. The New York property is good for what it cost me; and O'Sullivan hopes and expects to buy it back again. He has been in receipt of $7,500 per annum, since July, 1855. I shall probably send you two or three thousand dollars more; and, altogether, I should suppose I might count on the interest of nearly or quite $30,000. This would have seemed to me a fortune, five or six years ago; but our ideas change with our circumstances, and I now perceive that it is a bare competence. But the embroidery and trimmings shall come out of my inkstand.

Bridge called on Mr. Buchanan, on my behalf, and advised him of my intention to resign. The old fellow was very gracious and complimentary towards me, and said that I might take my own time. I presume my resignation is already in his hands, to take effect on the last day of August. It would not suit my arrangements to hold the office any longer.

We shall go to Paris, probably, in the course of September, and thence to Rome, viâ Marseilles, for the winter. I doubt whether you see us on your side of the water in less than two years from this coming summer; and if it were not for the children (who pine for America) I should consider myself a citizen of the world, and perhaps never come home. At all events, I feel no symptoms of homesickness as yet. There are few friends whom I should be most happy to meet again, however; and you rejoice me much by holding out a prospect (though a faint one) of your coming to England, this season.

We are all well.

Your friend,

Nath¹ Hawthorne.

Liverpool, March 20th, '57.

Dear Ticknor,

Miss Bacon's book seems to be ready, at last, and I send you a copy which will enable you to secure the copyright (doubtless invaluable) in America. She cut some passages out of my Preface, but did not otherwise alter it. The book grew above a hundred pages beyond its original size, in passing through the press. I hope you will sell so many copies that I shall not, at any rate, be quite ruined.

It will probably be published in London in the course of next week; and half or more of the edition will be transmitted to you as soon as possible.

Please to acknowledge the receipt of the copy now sent, in a note addressed to the Purser of the steamer Asia, care of E. Cunard, New York.

Mrs. Hawthorne and I, with Julian, are going to make a tour of Lincoln and elsewhere, next week, to be gone about a fortnight.

In haste,

Your friend,

Nath¹ Hawthorne.

Liverpool, April 9th, '57.

Dear Ticknor,

The 500 copies of Miss Bacon's book have been sent to me, ready for exportation; but the steamer cannot take them on Saturday, being already full-freighted. I shall send them either by the New York steamer, next week, or the Boston steamer in a fortnight — probably the latter, as I suppose the delay makes little difference, and it may be more convenient to you to receive them in Boston. They are in sheets. The London retail-price is 18/.

You will know what to charge in America. The 1000 copies, as they come from the printer's hands (exclusive of binding) have cost £238, 7, 9. "A fool and his money are soon parted." However, I do not repent what I have done; nor will I, even if I lose by it.

I enclose the items of a small amount paid by me for the relief of three Americans — a musician, a painter, and a teacher — who threw themselves on my tender mercies. I think it will be refunded, sooner or later. Mr. Tyng (whose drafts, you tell me, are not yet paid) had been shipwrecked, and absolutely needed the money which I advanced. His father will unquestionably pay it. Did you ever collect £30, or thereabouts, from an old Mr. Richardson, whom I sent home? I have a strong faith that he is an honest man.

I wonder what will become of all these vagabonds, when I quit the consulate! I doubt whether they find so good a friend in my successor; and yet I have never relieved anybody except when it would have been harsh and inhuman not to do it. The United States ought to make some provision for the relief of these people, in view of the propensity of our countrymen to stay abroad without means.

I think I have your disease, just at present — a spring fever, making me restless, sleepless, appetiteless, and wholly uncomfortable. I mean to take a trip to York with Mrs. Hawthorne, tomorrow.

Your friend,

Nath¹ Hawthorne.

Liverpool, April 24th, '57.

Dear Ticknor,

The books will go by this steamer, and I shall send therewith the necessary documents. The volume, as you say, is too big to meet with a ready sale. I expect to make a loss, and the only question is as to the more or less. With the exception of an unfavorable criticism in the Athenaeum, I know nothing of its success in England.

I enclose a critique of a volume of poems by Mrs. Howe; and the writer (Mr. Bright of this town) wished it to be sent to her. I read her play, (and thank you for it,) but her genius does not appear to be of the dramatic order. In fact, she has no genius or talent, except for making public what she ought to keep to herself — viz. her passions, emotions, and womanly weaknesses. "Passion Flowers" were delightful; but she ought to have been soundly whipt for publishing them.

Mrs. Hawthorne and I have made a pleasant trip to Yorkshire recently; and when the season is a little more advanced, we shall go to Lincolnshire. Scotland will occupy us at mid-summer; and then we shall go to London to remain till September, when we take our departure for the Continent. I shall leave the Consulate joyfully, but England with some regret; for it is a good country to live in, and if I were rich enough, I doubt whether I should ever leave it for a permanent residence elsewhere.

I have had to do some speechifying lately, having been toasted on a public occasion. I don't in the least admire my own oratory; but I do admire my pluck in speaking at all. I rather wonder at my coming off so well; but the reporters mar my eloquence most awfully. I am convinced that other orators write a fair copy of their speeches, and hand it to the reporters; and if I ever address an audience again, I mean to do the same.

It is now just about four years, I think, since you and I went to Washington together. It was a time of much enjoyment, especially of a liquid sort. I wish you would come across, and accompany us to the Continent.

Your edition of the Waverly Novels is very beautiful, and I agree with you that it has advantages over every other.

I believe I have nothing more to say at present.

Truly yours,

Nathl Hawthorne.

P. S.   I don't know what the jury may have decided in Mr. Kalloch's case, but I am just as sure he was guilty as if I had seen him in the fact.

P. S. 2d   I shall have to pay the Government two dollars for this invoice certificate, signed by myself!   Oh, the rascals!

Liverpool, May 8th, 1857.

Dear Ticknor,

I enclose a little due bill from the late Consul at Beyroot who finds himself short on his way home. He seems to be an honest man, and I think will call and pay it. He belongs in Concord, N. H.

I likewise send a manuscript document which will probably be called for by Mr. J. G. Palfrey.

Nothing new has happened since my last. Mrs. Hawthorne and I mean to make an expedition to Lincoln pretty soon. She and the children are very well.

I wish you would come over.

Your friend,

Nath¹ Hawthorne.

Liverpool, May 20th, 1857.

Dear Ticknor,

Your package reached me safely, after having been to London, and I hope you have got back our bag before this time. I am glad Mr. Tyng comes out so bright; indeed, I did not anticipate losing anything by him. As to old Mr. Richardson, I do not give him up yet.

Matters look dark, as regards Miss Bacon's book. I shall certainly not "save my bacon" there. It was absurd in me to let her publish such a heavy volume; and, in fact, I never thought of authorizing the publication of such an immense mass, which is enough to swamp a ship of the line. However, this shall be the last of my benevolent follies, and I never will be kind to anybody again as long as I live.

If there shall be opportunity to send by our bag, as heretofore, I want an elegantly bound copy (in the same style as the King of Portugal's, and Mr. Spiers) of the "House of the Seven Gables." If they *cannot* be sent by the bag, nor by any private conveyance, I do not want them.

Mrs. Hawthorne and I start on a trip to Lincolnshire &c, tomorrow. Would to Heaven you were with us! I want to see somebody from the "Corner."

Bennoch is going to the Continent with his wife, in a week or two. They have been removing from their house at Blackheath, to one nearer London.

I shall probably return from my tour just in time to write to you by the Boston steamer next after this.

Your friend,

Nath¹ Hawthorne.

Liverpool, June 5th, 1857.

Dear Ticknor,

Since my last, Mrs. Hawthorne and I have been on a very pleasant tour to some of the eastern counties of England, and returned only a day or two since. We went, among other places, to Boston, and really felt as if we were at home. There is a strong feeling of pride among the inhabitants in the greatness and prosperity of our American Boston, which they consider as the daughter of their old town. There is going to be a celebration, this summer, in honor of John Cotton, the first minister of our Boston; and Americans will be in great demand on the occasion. Our Boston ought to send a special representative.

I think Miss Bacon's book has fallen perfectly flat here. By the by, Mr. William H. Smith has demanded of me a retraction of my remarks about him in the preface; and it does appear that I did him injustice, so I shall give him a sugar-plum. If there had been any decent grounds for it, I would have tickled him still further, by way of keeping this unlucky book before the public eye.

Mrs. Hawthorne's health is very good indeed; and, in two or three weeks, we shall set out for Scotland. I have already been there once; but it is invariably my experience that second visits to a place are more agreeable and instructive than the first. Everything that I see in my travels goes down into my journal; and I have now hundreds of pages, which I would publish if the least of them were not too spicy. But Mrs. Hawthorne altogether excels me as a writer of travels. Her descriptions are the most perfect pictures that ever were put on paper; it is a pity they cannot be published; but neither she nor I would like to see her name on your list of female authors.

How is Grace Greenwood? I saw a paragraph in the Post, some months ago, stating that she had stabbed a man. If so, I suppose she may be now in the States Prison; but I think there must have been some mistake — at least, I hope so.

I observe that the President is offering my office among his friends, and that nobody seems desirous of accepting it. In fact, it is not very well worth acceptance, under the law that took effect from the first of January last; for that law cuts deeper than the former one into the fees that rightfully belong to the consul. I shall assert my right to these fees, and hold on to them, if possible; and perhaps the Auditor may allow them, either from a sense of justice, or more probably from ignorance or negligence. If I lose them, it will make a difference of some hundreds of pounds.

While I write this hasty scribble, I am sitting as a judge, or at least as a commissioner to take evidence; and the result will take effect in the Supreme Court of New York. I like these jobs;—they pay well, and our rascally Government cannot lay its finger on a shilling of the proceeds.

Truly yours,

Nath¹ Hawthorne.

Liverpool, July 30th, 1857.

Dear Ticknor,

Nothing important has happened lately; except that I have removed with my family from Southport to Manchester, where we shall probably remain till September. I sometimes feel as if I should like to have a home once more, and to be permanently settled from year's end to year's end; but that time is still far ahead. I wish I had a better house to come home to at last. What should you think of the expediency of investing some money in a place not very far from Boston, which I might occupy if I liked it, after my return; or which I might sell again without loss, if it did not suit me as a residence? And yet I don't quite like to think of giving up Concord; for my place there has many conveniences well adapted to my taste — especially the hill and wood behind the house, where I can take refuge from intruders, at any moment; a privilege which I mean to use pretty extensively. I have received, and been civil to, at least 10,000 visitors since I came to England; and I never wish to be civil to anybody again.

I have engaged Miss Ada Shepard (a graduate of Mr. Mann's College at Antioch) to take charge of my children while we remain on the Continent. She is recommended to me in the highest way, as respects acquirements and character; and it is essential to have some such person in order to give Mrs. Hawthorne the leisure and freedom which her health requires. I have tried English governesses, and find them ignorant and inefficient. Miss Shepard is to receive no salary, but only her expenses; and if she should apply to you for any money for her passage (as I shall advise her to do) you will oblige me by accepting her draft. I do not limit the amount, presuming that she will take only what is right. She is to cross, probably to Havre, in a sailing vessel, and will join us in Paris. As she wishes to perfect herself in the French pronunciation, she will perhaps reach Paris some time before our arrival, which I hope will be in the latter part of September.

I hear nothing about my successor, and begin to be rather anxious; — not that the office gives me any great trouble in the way I manage it at present; for I take my pleasure whenever and wherever I like, and get as well paid as if I slaved at the desk. But all my arrangements are made for quitting England, and I wish to be in Rome early in October.

I enclose a Bill of Lading of some articles which will arrive to your address by the Chatsworth. The contents of the packages are all truly stated; and as they are very nicely packed, Mrs. Hawthorne is anxious that the Custom House Inspectors should disturb them as little as possible. They ought to let them pass unopened. When you receive them, please to forward them to Concord. It gives me a slight sensation of home-sickness to be sending these things home; but I am pretty well contented to remain behind.

Your friend,

Nath¹ Hawthorne.

P. S. The freight of my goods is unpaid. Of course, you will pay the carriage to Concord on my account.

Liverpool, Aug. 29th, 1857.

Dear Ticknor,

No news yet of my successor; not even of his appointment. I have been well enough contented to wait hitherto, because I live at Uncle Sam's expense, and do him very little service — the old scoundrel! But it is getting late in the season, and I ought to be in Italy in little more than a month. I shall write again to the Department by next steamer, and shall press as earnestly for a dismissal as most people do for an appointment. If I should be kept here through the winter, it would delay my return to America another year; for I must spend two seasons on the Continent, at any rate.

We are still living at Manchester, and I pass back and forth two or three times a week.

In a hurry,

Truly yours,

Nath¹ Hawthorne.

Liverpool, Sept. 26th, '57.

Dear Ticknor,

I thought I should have been in Paris by this time; but I was telegraphed back from Leamington on account of the severe illness of Mr. Wilding, who is prostrated with a nervous fever, attended with delirium. This has thrown a load of business upon me, making it impossible for me to leave at present. The worst effect of [it] is (so far as I am concerned) that it will cause an embarrassing delay in the adjustment of my accounts, and the arrangement of my financial concerns. I can see my own way through, however.

I had a letter from the new Consul per last steamer. He is to leave New York tomorrow, and nobody will pray for his safe passage and speedy arrival more sincerely than I shall. You may be sure I shall lend him no money nor back him up with any responsibility; indeed, he will immediately find himself in possession of funds (not his own, to be sure) that will put him beyond the necessity of fleecing anybody but Uncle Sam. To that I have no objection, provided his own conscience will permit him.

I think I have nothing more to say. Good-bye,

Your friend,

N. H.

Liverpool, October 9th, 1857.

Dear Ticknor,

Here I am, writing you one more scribble from the old place. Mr. Tucker arrived by the Baltic, but could not take the office immediately, his Exequatur not being out. He will come in on Monday, and then I shall draw freer breath than for many a day past. Mr. Wilding being ill, and Mr. Pearce so nervous that he can hardly speak or stand, I have had a heavy burthen on my shoulders; but a man never knows what he can do till he is put to it. Mr. Wilding's illness has most seriously inconvenienced me by the delay of my accounts; for they are of a peculiar class, and it has been necessary to instruct another person how to make them up without aid or advice from him;

and he held all the clues in his hands. However, this difficulty is in a fair way to be surmounted; and I shall soon know how I stand with the Treasury Department.

Wilding has run a narrow chance for his life, which was at one time despaired of. He is now on the recovery; and Mr. Tucker has promised to give him the place of vice-consul, which will be vacated by Mr. Pearce, who retires with me.

The new consul will be very popular with the shipmasters and American residents; a bluff, jolly, good natured gentleman, fond of society, and an excellent companion — wholly unlike me in every possible respect. * * * We have met in a most agreeable way, and seem to like one another vastly.

I have long heard rumors from the knowing ones here of the terrible crisis that was coming in the finances of the United States. Very likely, some of my investments may suffer; for the trouble seems to come down like an avalanche. If there were any ready cash to be had, I should think it would be a first-rate time to buy a place to live in; but I leave everything to your judgment, being sure that you have done, and will do, all for the best. Mrs. Hawthorne and the children are still at Leamington, and our new American governess has joined them there. She seems to prove entirely satisfactory.

I shall enclose you a bill of lading of another large box of books, and miscellaneous articles, which I hope will meet with the same favor from the Collector as those which have already been sent; and for which I beg you to convey to him my best thanks. You may assure him on my part, that these articles are all for our own use, and none of them dutiable to the best of my belief. The books are not new; some of them were brought from America; others have been presented to me here; and all have been used. There is a writing desk in the box, and private papers &c &c &c.

We shall make no long stay in Paris, but go almost immediately to Italy, viâ Marseilles; unless, indeed, Italy should be in a commotion before we can get there. There are many signs of an outbreak.

I shall continue to write to you frequently by
mail; and you must do the same by me.

Your friend,   N. Hawthorne.

P. S. Old Cass has sent me a despatch,
referring to mine, and bearing testimony to the
"prudence and efficiency" of my official conduct.

10, Landsdown Circus,

Leamington, Nov. 5th, 1857.

Dear Ticknor,

Yours of October 21st, (I think,) enclosing
the letter of credit, was received a day or two
ago. I have not yet needed the credit, and am
in hopes not to have to use it for some time to
come; but the continued illness of Mr. Wilding
has thus far prevented me from understanding
precisely how the balance stands between myself and the Treasury Department. I had a
narrow escape from being involved in a serious
embarrassment by the stoppage of the Liverpool
Borough Bank; having drawn out funds to a
large amount (owing to a rumor that had reached

me) only a short time previously. What a bother it is to have any money to take care of!

We are going to London early next week, and I suppose we shall have to remain there at least a fortnight, and perhaps more, before it will be possible for me to leave England. I expected to have been in Rome before this date, but should be well enough contented to be in London, if this wet autumnal weather were not so unfavorable to Mrs. Hawthorne's health. She continues pretty well, however, and I hope will not suffer seriously from the delay.

I understand that Mr. Alcott (of whom I bought the Wayside) has bought a piece of land adjacent to mine, and two old houses on it. I remember the situation as a very pretty one; and I do not doubt that those two old houses might be converted into a domicile that would just suit me. If he should swamp himself by his expenditures on this place, I should be very glad to take it off his hands; and it seems to me highly probable (judging from the character of the man) that he will ultimately be glad to have me do so. The matter may be ripe by the time we get back to America; but I should feel much more inclined to come home if I had the prospect of a more convenient house to come to. You would oblige me by having an eye to this.

As regards the announcement of a book, I am not quite ready for it yet. If I could be perfectly quiet for a few months, I have no doubt that something would result; but I shall have so much to see while I remain in Europe, that I think I must confine myself to keeping a journal. Unless I return home next summer, however, I shall make a serious effort to produce something.

I heard from Bennoch a few days ago, but have not seen him this long while. The commercial men seem to be in almost as much trouble here as on your side of the water. Good-bye.

Your friend,

Nath¹ Hawthorne.

You had better direct to me at the consulate until further advices.

Hôtel dû Louvre, Paris,

Jany 7th, 1858.

Dear Ticknor,

You will be sorry to hear that I was detained in England until the day before yesterday, by the impossibility of getting my complicated accounts ready at an earlier date. They wind up, however, better than I expected, leaving a balance of at all events about two hundred pounds in my favor, which will be twice that amount if Government settles with me on the basis which I think just.

We staid at Leamington till the beginning of November, and have been ever since in London, where all the children had the measles, and Mrs. Hawthorne suffered a good deal from illness. However, we saw and enjoyed a good deal, in spite of difficulties and troubles!

I have seen our poor friend Bennoch several times, and find him still the same warm-hearted and excellent fellow that he was during his prosperity. Nevertheless, he feels his misfortunes very sensibly, though he bears them like a man. I do not know (nor, I think, does he)

what he means to do, after the business shall
be finally wound up. I advised him to think of
going to America, where he has so many
friends; for, you know, it [is] almost a hopeless
business for a ruined man ever to recover himself in England. He spent the evening with
us, last Monday, and bade me tell Fields and
yourself that he is not dead yet, though beaten
down.

We reached Paris last night, by way of
Boulogne. The weather is terribly cold, and
we find it difficult to keep ourselves from freez-
ing, by these wretched little wood-fires. Indeed, I find how English I have grown, in
five years past, by my antipathy to French
fires, and everything else that is French.

You will next hear from me in Rome, and
meanwhile may direct your letters to Pakenham, Hooker & Co, Bankers, at that place.

In haste

Your friend,   N. H.

Rome, April 14th, 1858.

Dear Ticknor,

I received your letter in due season, and
have been intending to write to you; but the
languor and laziness of the Roman atmosphere
have prevented me. The climate does not seem
to suit me at all, and I have hardly been free
from cold a single day since my arrival. We
shall stay here about a month longer, and then
proceed to Florence for the summer, with the
purpose of returning to Rome to spend another
winter — after which, I suppose I must turn my
face homeward. I doubt greatly whether I
shall be able to settle down to serious literary
labor as long as I remain abroad; at all events,
not in Italy. In England, if not interrupted by
other avocations, I could have worked to good
purpose.

We find living in Rome quite as expensive,
in most particulars, as it was in England. Rent
is a good deal dearer; and nothing is cheaper
except maccaroni, figs, bad cigars, and sour
wine. Rome struck me very disagreeably at
first, but rather improves upon acquaintance,

and has a sort of fascination which will make
me reluctant to take a final leave of it. I wish
I were a little more patriotic; but to confess
the truth, I had rather be a sojourner in any
other country than return to my own. The
United States are fit for many excellent pur-
poses, but they certainly are not fit to live in.

Miss Lauder, a lady from my native town,
has made an excellent bust of me, of which I
will enclose a photograph, if I can get one.
Even Mrs. Hawthorne is delighted with it, and,
as a work of art, it has received the highest
praise from all the sculptors here, including
Gibson, the English sculptor, who stands at the
head of the profession. Miss Bremer declares
it to be the finest modelled bust she ever saw.
I tell you this in the hope that you and Fields
may do what may be in your power to bring
Miss Lauder's name favorably before the public; for she is coming back to America (for the
summer only) and might be greatly benefitted
by receiving commissions for busts &c. &c.
She is a very nice person, and I like her exceedingly. If you happen to see her, she will give

you the latest and most authentic news of me and mine.

I think I told you, in a former letter, that I intended that N. C. Peabody, my wife's brother, should take the land at the Wayside, after the expiration of Mr. Bull's lease, at the beginning of the present month. I do not know whether any previous notice to Mr. Bull was necessary, though I presume not, unless it is so stipulated in the lease. I enclose a note for Mr. Bull, which please to send.

Do write yourself, and tell Fields to write, as a matter of Christian charity.

Your friend, Nath¹ Hawthorne.

Direct me still to the care of Pakenham & Hooker, Bankers, Rome.

Rome, March 4th, 1859.

Dear Ticknor,

I thank you sincerely for your letter of the 8th ult.; and I suppose you, or Fields, have by this time got mine of the 3d. Since then, nothing of much importance has happened, unless it be that I was, for a short time, confined to my bed. This Roman climate is really terrible, and nobody can be sure of life or health from one day to another. The utmost caution is requisite, in regard to diet, and exposure to air; and after all the care that can be taken, there is a lurking poison in the atmosphere that will be likely enough to do your business. I never knew that I had either bowels or lungs, till I came to Rome; but I have found it out now, to my cost. For the present, however, we are all pretty well, and are rejoicing in the prospect of leaving this pestilential city on the 15th of next month.

It is our calculation to set sail from Liverpool in the course of July next — probably by the steamer of the first of that month. My wife's brother is to leave the Wayside, in season for us to get into it immediately. We have written to him, that, if he will engage some person to do the necessary work in the garden, we will arrange about the payment. Would you do me the favor to communicate with him on this matter? Tell him I have asked you to pay whatever amount may be necessary for manure, labor, or other expenses he may authorize on the garden.

I feel in somewhat better spirits to come home, because I think I see how an addition may be made to the house, which need not be enormously expensive, and yet will afford us the necessary space. I want a drawing-room, two bed-chambers, and two chambers for servants, in addition to what we now have; and these, if I mistake not, I can get by adding on a wing to the southern end of the house. I should be very reluctant to leave Concord, or to live anywhere else than by my own hillside; that one spot (always excepting the old 'Corner Store') is the only locality that attaches me to my native land. I am tied to it by one of my heartstrings, all the rest of which have long ago broken loose.

I told you in my last, that I had written a Romance. It still requires a good deal of revision, trimming off of exuberances, and filling up of vacant spaces; but I think it will be all right in a month or two after I arrive. I shall do my best upon it, you may be sure; for

I feel that I shall come before the public, after so long an interval, with all the uncertainties of a new author. If I were only rich enough, I do not believe I should ever publish another book, though I might continue to write them for my own occupation and amusement. But, with a wing of a house to build, and my girls to educate, and Julian to send to Cambridge, I see little prospect of the '*dolce far niente*,' as long as there shall be any faculty left in me. I have another Romance ready to be written, as soon as this one is off the stocks.

General Pierce has been spending the winter in Naples, where he is still detained on account of his wife's health; so that I have not yet met him, and very likely our meeting may be deferred till we both are home again. There are said to be 1500 Americans now in Rome.

We are now in the height of the Carnival, and the young people find it great fun. To say the truth, so do I; but I suppose I should have enjoyed it still better at twenty. The Prince of Wales is here, and seems to take vast delight in pelting and being pelted, along the

Corso. The poor fellow will not have many such merry times, in his future life.

Do you hear anything of Bennoch? I have received only one letter from him, since leaving England, and have hardly the heart to write to him, for I greatly fear that there is no possibility of his ever retrieving his fortunes. It is a great pity.

It will not be worth while to direct another letter to me at Rome, after receiving this, tho' it is just possible that one might find me here. We shall spend perhaps a fortnight in Venice, and, if necessary, you might write thither, *poste restante.* My next address will be Hottinger & Co, Bankers, Paris. It seems but a week or two, now, before I shall shake hands with you in America!

Your friend,
Nathl Hawthorne.

Rome, May 23d, 1859.

Dear Ticknor,

It is a very long while, I believe, since I have written, and certainly very long since I

heard from you. Meanwhile, we have suffered
a great deal of trouble and anxiety from Una's
illness; and, at one period, we had scarcely no
hope of ever taking her out of Rome. Indeed,
the physician did not encourage us to think
that she would live even from one day to
another. She has been restored to us, however,
and, for several weeks past, has steadily and
rapidly gained strength; and the Doctor now
assures us that she will be stronger and healthier
than ever before in her life. God's providence
and a good constitution (for I attribute little
efficacy to homeopathic remedies) have brought
her through. Had it been otherwise, I doubt
whether we should ever have had the heart to
come home without her.

It has been necessary for us to remain in
Rome longer than we intended, while Una was
getting strong enough to travel. The Doctor
now says that she may safely set out, but ad-
vises us to spend some little time on the seashore. We shall therefore take the railway to
Civita Vecchia (forty miles from Rome) and
thence go by steamer to Leghorn, where we

mean to spend ten days or a fortnight. By that time, we hope, Una will be quite able to bear the fatigues of travelling; and we shall go by steamer to Marseilles, thence by railway to Geneva, and, after a brief visit to Switzerland, shall turn towards Paris. It had been my purpose to sail from England for home as early as the first of July; and, in spite of all of these impediments, I do not mean to be delayed much beyond that date. You will see us before the end of summer.

Rome is very quiet, and the war on the frontier of Sardinia causes us no inconvenience here. We shall go a little nearer the seat of hostilities, at Leghorn, but we have no apprehension of difficulty or disturbance. The rush of strangers from Italy, however, has been very great; and I imagine lodgings will be very cheap here, next season.

Remember me kindly to all my friends. I shall be delighted to see you all again; but I will fairly own that it is not altogether agreeable to think of coming back, after so long an absence as mine. I am afraid I have lost my country by staying away too long.

I enclose (to save postage) a letter from Una to her Aunt. You can read it, if you please, as it gives some account of her illness; and then please to enclose it to Miss Elizabeth M. Hawthorne, care of John Dike, Esq. Salem.

Gen¹ Pierce spent a month or two here, and left for Vienna, some weeks ago. I suppose he will be in Paris by this time. He has not decided whether to return home, this year. Mr. Motley and family are still here, but will start for Paris next week. Our friend C. G. Thompson is about returning to Boston with his family. He has wonderfully improved since his residence here, and is now a very exquisite artist, but, I fear, not a very successful one. He deserves success, and I wish you, and Fields, and Whipple, and other kind hearted people, would make some little flourish of trumpets on his return. A few paragraphs in the newspapers would be efficacious in giving him a fresh start, and a little popular sunshine is what he needs to make him flower out.

We leave Rome the 25th—that is, the day after to-morrow.

Your friend,

Nath¹ Hawthorne.

Leamington, Oct. 6th, 59.

Dear Ticknor,

I was very glad to receive your note of 20th Sept, and a little ashamed for not having written for so long a time. But I am never a very good correspondent; and for nearly three months past, I have been constantly occupied with my book, which required more work to be done upon it than I supposed. I am now, I think, within a fortnight of finishing it. There will be three English volumes, or two of yours, each perhaps as big as the Seven Gables. Mrs. Hawthorne (the only person who has read it) speaks very much in its favour; but I sometimes suspect that she has a partiality for the author. I have not yet decided upon the title.

Smith & Elder have signed an agreement to publish the book, and pay me £600 on the assignment of the copyright. It will, I suppose, certainly be ready for the press in the course of this month, (at furthest, by the end of it,) and these £600 will preclude the necessity of your remitting any money through the Barings. By-the-by, speaking of money matters, I should like to have some brief estimate of how much property I possess. If I find that I can prudently do it, I should be glad to spend some money before leaving England, in books and other matters.

I have heard nothing of Fields for some weeks past, but hope soon to hear of his return from the Continent. I do not intend to send the manuscript of the book to Smith & Elder till he comes back, as he has had the whole management of the business. No doubt, he will make arrangements about your having the sheets with a view to simultaneous publication.

We have been spending the summer, since the middle of July, at Redcar, a little watering place on the shore of the German ocean. It was the most secluded spot I ever met with, and therefore very favorable to literary labor.

We had not a single visitor or caller, while we were there. This suited Mrs. Hawthorne as well as myself; for she was quite worn out with her anxiety and watching, during Una's illness. Her health is now considerably improved; and Una herself is as plump and rosy as any English girl. We are all very well, considering what some of us have gone through.

You will see us, probably, by the end of June next. I must confess that I have out-lived all feeling of homesickness; but still there are some friends whom I shall be rejoiced to see again — and none more than yourself. I doubt whether I shall ever again be contented to live long in one place, after the constant changes of residence for nearly seven years past. I am much troubled about our house in Concord; it is not big enough for us, and is hardly worth repairing and enlarging.

I think we may probably spend the winter here in Leamington, as it is a very pleasant town, with many conveniences for transitory residents. You had better, however, continue to send your letters (when you write any, which

I hope will be oftener than of late) through the Barings. I have only received one letter from you since we left Rome.

I write with a horrible pen; as you see; but, such as it is, it has served me to write my whole book with. Believe me

most sincerely yours

Nath. Hawthorne.

Leamington, Dec. 1st, '59.

Dear Ticknor,

It is a good while since I heard from you; but I make no complaints, being myself so dilatory a correspondent.

I finished the Romance some weeks ago; and Smith & Elder wrote to me that it was in the printers hands, and would pass speedily through the press. Since then, I have heard nothing about the matter, and I cannot account for the delay, except on the supposition that they mean to put off the publication till the spring. This, indeed, seems to me the most eligible course; because it would be quite impossible to make the necessary arrangements for the simultaneous publication on your side of the water, supposing the book to appear in this country at Christmas.

By Fields' advice, I gave the book the title of "The Romance of Monte Beni"; but as Smith & Elder thought it not a captivating name, I sent them several others to choose from. I do not [know] which they will select; but their choice need not govern yours, and, if you wish to announce the book, I should like to have you call it "Saint Hilda's Shrine." We can change the title afterwards, should it appear advisable.

The publication of the Romance being deferred, I cannot call upon Smith & Elder to pay over the £600, at present; so that you would oblige me by lodging £200, or thereabouts, with the Barings.

I had a letter from Fields, about a week ago. He is still in Paris, and seems to have given up the idea of spending the winter in Italy.

We hear from Bennoch occasionally, and are

in hopes of seeing him here, in the course of a few days.

When we were at Marseilles, last June, I left three trunks in charge of our consul there, to be transmitted to the United States, directed to your care. They contained clothing, books, and curiosities and works of art, which we collected in Rome. I gave directions to have them sent to Boston; but it is possible, if no vessel offered for that port, that they might go to New York. In either case, no doubt, you would be notified of their arrival. If they have been received, I wish you would let me know; and, if not, you would greatly oblige me by writing to our consul at Marseilles on that subject. His name is Derbé, I think, or some such French name; but you would find it in a blue-book, or United States Register.

Please to pay any bills that come to you, certified by Mrs. Horace Mann, for repairs on the house at Concord. I wish I had a better house, and I should enjoy far greater pleasure in the idea of coming home. As the case stands, I have hardly any other anticipation

so pleasant as that of seeing you at the old
'Corner Store.'

We are all very well, and heartily hope that
you are the same.

Your friend,

Nath¹ Hawthorne.

Leamington, Decr 22d, '59.

Dear Ticknor,

I have received proof-sheets of the Romance
as far as the commencement of the second volume. They were going at the rate of 50 pages
a day; and I was afraid they would get the
book out, on this side of the water, before
Christmas, without waiting for you to get it
through the press and publish simultaneously.
So I suggested that there was no occasion for
haste, inasmuch as I should remain in England
till next summer. The printing has since gone
on much more leisurely.

The exact middle of the work is at the 10th
chapter (called "the Pedigree of Monte Beni")

of the second volume; and you must commence your second volume with that chapter.

The Publishers proposed to call the Romance "The Transformation; or the Romance of Monte Beni"; but this title did not suit me, and I rejected it. I think I shall call it "The Marble Faun"; and unless I write you to the contrary, I wish you would prefix that title on the title-page.

It is a good while since I heard from Fields. Bennoch has been promising us a visit here, but probably will not now come till after Christmas.

We are all pretty well.

As the delay in publishing the Romance will prevent my receiving the £600 at present, I wish you [would] place funds to some moderate amount with the Barings. I don't know how my account stands with them.

I long to see you, and all my friends, and am at last beginning to be homesick.

Sincerely yours,

Nath¹ Hawthorne.

P. S. No letters from you this long while.

Leamington, Jany 26th, 1860.

Dear Ticknor,

Your letter arrived yesterday, and was very welcome, after so long a silence.

The printers are now nearly at the end of the third volume of the Romance, but I presume the publishers will not think of bringing it out at present. I wrote to Smith & Elder, not long since, to remind them of the necessity of a simultaneous publication on both sides of the water. They replied that they had already sent you the proof-sheets of the first volume, and would duly forward the remainder, and would also let you know the time of publication here.

I think I told you that your second volume should begin with the 10th chapter of the 2d volume of the English edition, entitled "The Pedigree of Monte Beni." Each of the three volumes has about 290 pages.

I cannot think of a better title than "The Marble Faun"; and I hope you will call it so:—"The Marble Faun; or the Romance of Monte Beni." Smith & Elder do not seem to be decided, as yet, on this point; but I am well assured that the above title will suit the American public better than any which these English booksellers are likely to substitute for it; nor is there any reason, that I know of, why the book should not have two titles in two countries.

We are passing rather a dull winter here; for the cloudy, chill, and rainy weather leaves us little inclination to make excursions, and, besides, Mrs. Hawthorne's health is not so good, in this damp atmosphere, as it was in Rome. I shall really be glad to get home, although I do not doubt I shall be tortured with life-long wishes to cross the sea again. I fear I have lost the capacity of living contentedly in any one place.

I want to spend some money in books and other things before my return. How much can I afford? Anything? Very little, I fear; but I should be glad if you could give me some approximate idea of what my investments amount to. But do not put yourself to any trouble about it.

I heard from Fields, two or three weeks since, when he was on the point of starting for

Italy. I suppose you will be taking your turn for a visit to Europe, as soon as he returns; and certainly you deserve some recreation after so much labour.

Bennoch sent his remembrances to us, at Christmas, in the shape of a barrel of oysters; since which I have not seen or heard from him.

I will write again, when I hear anything definite about the publication of the Romance.

Affectionately yours,

Nath¹ Hawthorne.

Leamington, Feby 3d, '60.

Dear Ticknor,

Smith & Elder tell me that they shall send you the sheets of the 3d volume by this steamer and shall bring the book out on the 28th inst. Supposing the former volumes to have come seasonably to hand, this will doubtless allow you time to get the work out simultaneously; otherwise, the consequences may be rather awkward.

Smith & Elder are determined to take a title out of their own heads, though they affirm that it was originally suggested by me, "Transformation." I beseech you not to be influenced by their bad example. Call it "The Marble Faun; a Romance of Monte Beni." If you are in any doubt about it, ask Whipple to read the book, and choose or make a title for it; — but do not let it be "Transformation."

Give copies to Whipple, Hillard, Longfellow, and others whom you know to be friends of the author. Give one to Elizabeth Peabody; send one to my sister, care of John Dike, Esq. Salem; — also one to David Roberts, Esq, Counsellor at Law, Salem, and to William B. Pike, Esq, Collector, Salem. I can think of no others at this moment. Of course, Gen¹ Pierce is to have one; Lowell, too. In short, you know pretty well who are the persons whom I should like to please, and who would be gratified by a presentation copy.

In haste,

Your friend,

Nath¹ Hawthorne.

P. S. I saw Bennoch the other day, and am going to dine with him in Coventry tomorrow. I think I shall spend two or three months in the vicinity of London, between now and the latter part of June, when I purpose sailing.

Leamington, Feby 10th, '60.

Dear Ticknor,

Yours of the 26th ult. is this morning received; and I am surprised that the first volume of the Romance had not sooner reached you. Smith & Elder told me that they had sent it as early as the 6th January. I should have objected to their publishing so early as the 28th inst, but they did not give me notice of their design until after they had sent off the 3d volume, and made all their arrangements. I fear you will be pressed for time; but if you bring out your edition before the importation of any copies of the English one, it will save the copyright. This will give you a whole week, or more, in March. Moreover, if your first edition consists only of a single copy, it will guard the copyright as well as if it were

ten thousand. If the whole work should not
be ready, you could publish the first volume.

I am ,fully determined not to retain their
absurd title of "Transformation." Let it be
"The Marble Faun; a Romance of Monte
Beni," unless Whipple (if he will do me the
kindness to set his wits to work upon the
matter) should think of a better.

If you have an opportunity, by any person
going to Rome, I wish you would send William
W. Story a copy. If I could bring any public
notice upon his sculptural productions (which
are shamefully neglected) I should feel that I
had done a good thing.

Fields means to come home in the same
steamer with me; and it is my purpose to sail
in the latter part of June. I long to be at
home, and yet I can hardly anticipate much
pleasure in returning, when I consider the miserable confusion in which you are involved. I
go for a dissolution of the Union; and, on that
ground, I hope the Abolitionists will push
matters to extremity.

I should be very glad to send you an article

for the Atlantic Monthly, but I see little hope of being able to do it, at present. I have lost the habit of writing magazine articles, and it would take me a long while and very favorable circumstances, to get into a proper fix for such compositions. I have many proposals from magazines on this side of the water, but shall certainly decline them all, and listen to nobody but yourself. It is possible that some good idea may occur to me, and, if so, I will do my best to take advantage of it.

I have come to the conclusion that New England is the healthiest country in the world. Everybody here has one sort of sickness or another, throat-complaints being the most prevalent. Mrs. Hawthorne has been confined to her bed for some weeks past, by a severer access of her old bronchial complaint. The Doctor speaks favorably of her case; but I shall be rejoiced when we leave England.

As soon as Mrs. H. is able to move, I intend to take my family to Blackheath, or somewhere else in the neighborhood of London, there to remain till the time of sailing.

All the advantages of residing in England are concentrated in London. Leave out that, and I would rather be in America — that is to say, if Presidential elections and all other political turmoil could be done away with — and if I could but be deprived of my political rights, and left to my individual freedom. The sweetest thing connected with a foreign residence is, that you have no rights and no duties, and can live your own life without interference of any kind. I shall never again be so free as I have been in England and Italy.

Truly yours,

Nath¹ Hawthorne.

Leamington, March 9th, '60.

Dear Ticknor,

Barings advise me of £100 remitted by you not long ago; and as there had been a previous £100, and as Smith & Elder have paid over the £600, I am fully provided with funds till I see you again.

I am sorry you have been so much hurried about the book. It came out in London at the time appointed, and seems to have gone off pretty well, for Smith & Elder wrote me, some days ago, that their edition was nearly exhausted, and that they were about printing another. As everybody complains that the mysteries of the story are not sufficiently accounted for, I intend to add a few pages to the concluding chapter, in order to make things a little clearer. The additional matter, when written, shall be sent you in manuscript.

I think there would have been no danger, in a legal point of view, in changing the title of the Romance; and I therefore hope you will have called it "The Marble Faun." But, after all, it is of no essential consequence.

I thank you for the number of the Atlantic, which seems to me a good one; also for the newspapers. The only American papers that I have seen, for nearly a year, are those which you have sent me; but I shall see enough of them in a few months more.

I have a letter from Fields this morning,

dated at Rome on 2d of this month. He pur-
poses leaving Rome in a few days, and will
probably be here early in April, at farthest. I
have engaged passages for him and my own
family at one of three dates — June 2d, 16th,
or 30th, — most probably we shall sail on the
16th; but if he chooses to come at an earlier
date, it will be in his power. For my part, I
absolutely long to be at home, and if an earlier
voyage would be comfortable, I should certainly
prefer it. I shall enjoy nothing, till I have
touched my native soil again.

Mrs. Hawthorne is quite comfortable now, in
point of health; except that she feels the raw-
ness of the English atmosphere very sensibly.
All the rest of the family are well.

I went up to London, the other day, and
found Bennoch in good trim. He says that
the past year has been very favorable to him
in his business relations; and I hope we shall
yet see him as prosperous as formerly.

We shall soon remove from Leamington, but
are in doubt whether to establish ourselves for
a month or two at Bath, or in the neighborhood

of London. Spring, in any part of England, is the worst portion of the year.

Your friend,

Nath¹ Hawthorne.

13, Charles Street,
Bath, April 6th, '60.

Dear Ticknor,

I have received the three copies of The Marble Faun; and I wish, whenever you print the concluding pages (which I transmitted several weeks ago), you would send me another copy, if you can find the means so to do. I want it for Bennoch. Your edition is certainly much handsomer than the English one—at exactly a fifth of the price!

I have been much gratified by the kind feeling and generous praise contained in the notices you send me. After so long absence and silence, I like to be praised too much. It sounds like a welcome back among my friends. But, in fact, if I have written anything well, it should be this Romance; for I have never thought or felt more deeply, or taken more pains. So far as I can judge, its success in England has been good. Smith & Elder published their second edition a week or two ago, and I daily receive notes of congratulation and requests for autographs — which latter annoyance seems to be the great and ultimate result of literary reputation. I scarcely thought that these fat-brained Englishmen would have taken so wild a fiction in such good part. To say the truth, some of them do grumble awfully; for it is not every man that knows how to read a Romance; and if I were not myself the author, I doubt whether I should like this one.

It is very long since I heard anything from Fields — not since February, I think, while he was still in Rome. Where can he be? If I leave England without him, you need never expect to see him again; for he certainly will not return, unless in somebody's custody. You had better stop his supplies, after the middle of June. For my part, I already begin to count the days that intervene between now and our departure, and we are all restless and feverish with the thought of home. I cannot promise to be contented when I get there, after becoming habituated to such constant change; but I mean to try to settle down into a respectable character, and have serious thoughts of going to meeting every Sunday forenoon.

If you happen to hear of a puppy-dog, of a large and good breed, I should like to get such a one.

If I find myself respectably off, as to funds, I shall begin to make an addition of two or three rooms to my house, as soon as we get back. It was small enough, in all conscience, when we left it; and now the children (who used to be bundled together in one room) will require separate apartments. I really don't see how we are to live in it; but we all have an attachment to the spot, and have looked upon it always as our ultimate home; so that, poor as it is, I should prefer it to a better one.

I am going to London soon, for a week or two, but shall leave Mrs. Hawthorne and the children here. My wife's health is much improved by the air of Bath, and I do not doubt the atmosphere and quiet of Concord will quite restore her.

I think I have nothing more to say, at present.
Your friend,
Nathl Hawthorne.

Bath, 19th April, '60.
Dear Ticknor,

Yours of the 3d inst. has come to hand, and also the newspapers, and the Atlantic for May, for all of which I thank you. This number of the Atlantic promises to be particularly good, both as regards poetry and prose.

I am glad the Romance has gone off so well. Here, it may also be called a successful affair; Smith & Elder having got out their third edition, and perhaps more by this time; for the good opinion of the "Times" has great weight with John Bull.

Just now, however, the English public cares very little for any American except John Heenan, the prize-fighter. You cannot imagine the interest that is felt in the battle, nor their surprise at Heenan's standing up so sturdily against their champion. No moral or intellectual triumph, that we could possibly win, would inspire them with half the respect, or half the mortification, that the loss of this fight would have caused them. It is, indeed, a great pity that it was left undecided — that is, provided (as there were ten chances to one) the event had turned out favorably for our side. You see, having lived so long among Englishmen, I have grown to be almost as great a fool as themselves.

I still hear nothing from Fields, nor do I know how to direct a letter to him. Unless he turns up soon, I shall have to relinquish the state-room which I took for him and his wife in the steamer of 16th June. My own purpose to sail at that date is decided, and I long for the time to come. All my homesickness has fallen on me at once, and even Julian is scarcely more impatient than myself.

I shall pay a parting visit to London in the course of next month, where I mean to pass a quiet week or two, leaving Mrs. Hawthorne and the children here. Mrs. Hawthorne has been very well, till a few days ago, when she caught a cold by sitting down, in the open air, and is now confined to her bed. In my opinion, America is the healthiest and safest country to live in, in the world. There are more delightful atmospheres, perhaps, than that of New England, but none that has so little mischief in it. I look upon it quite as a Paradise, but am afraid I may change my opinion, after a few months' trial. But I shall do my best to live contentedly at home.

I don't know whether I remembered to ask you to send a copy of The Marble Faun to General Pierce; but, of course, you will have done it.

Your friend,

Nath¹ Hawthorne.

Concord, June 28th, Thursday.

Dear Ticknor,

We arrived here safely, and are established in our little house, and as comfortable as can be imagined.

Mr. Emerson has just called, and says he will not be able to come to your dinner, if it is to take place as soon as Monday — inasmuch as he is to go to Ohio for a week. It would also be more convenient for me to come to Boston some little time hence. Could the dinner be put off a week or so?

In a great hurry,

    Your friend,

        Nath¹ Hawthorne.

P. S. Act as you think best about the dinner. I shall be ready at any moment — only, pray don't let it take the form of a banquet in my honour! You will think me vain for apprehending any such thing.

        N. H.

Dear Ticknor,

The enclosed note from Mrs. Hawthorne refers to an overcoat of Julian's, which was left at Halifax, and which the stewardess promised to get back. Will you be kind enough to have it delivered?

I am enjoying myself with your cigars, which are very good.

Your friend,

Nath¹ Hawthorne.

Concord, Sept. 27th, '60.

Dear Ticknor,

    or Dear Fields,

I am in great need of $50; and the case being urgent, I wish you would send it by the Concord expressman (Adams) so that I may get it on Friday evening. Would it not be practicable, hereafter, to give me a credit to some moderate amount on the Bank in this place; so that I need not be continually bothering you for money?

Una seems entirely well; her case having yielded at once to the incantations of a certain electrical witch. This Doctress says that the crisis was a most fortunate one, and that without it she would have been subject to life-long disease.

Your friend,

Nath¹ Hawthorne.

Concord, Oct 3d, '60.

Dear Ticknor,

$500 is just the sum to begin with.

Una, I am happy to say, appears perfectly well. From henceforth, forever, I shall recommend medical electricity for all diseases. Driscoll had better try it. Mrs. Rollins of Cambridge is the doctress.

I am glad that you took a little time for recreation, and only wish I could have been with you.

Your friend,

Nath¹ Hawthorne.

P. S. My house begins to make a good appearance.

Concord, October 29th, '60.

Dear Ticknor,

I have a bill for timber and other building materials to pay, amounting to 484 dollars, or thereabouts; and I wish you would send me another check for $500, available at the Concord Bank. I have still some of the former $500 remaining, but want to reserve it to draw upon at need. I should like this money in a day or two, if convenient.

I have a bad cold, which I caught in coming home, last Saturday.

Your friend,

Nath¹ Hawthorne.

Concord, Nov. 23d, 1860.

Dear Ticknor,

I have given Burchmore an order on you for $50. Pay it, and I promise you not to trouble you again on his account. It is impossible not to assist an old acquaintance in distress — for once, at least.

Your friend,

Nath¹ Hawthorne.

P. S.   Do not write to me about this; for I do not wish my wife to know how I throw away my money.

Concord, Novr 17th, 1860.

Dear Ticknor,

We bought a carpet at Chipman's, Hanover St., price $32.23. The bill will probably be sent you; and if the amount is as above stated, you would oblige me by paying it. I enclose a bill for marble fireplaces; and shall take the liberty to tell the dealer to call on you for payment. If ever I can repay you for all this trouble by taking charge of your business, you may command me; but I doubt whether you would be quite as well satisfied with my administration as I am with yours.

Your friend
(in haste)
Nath¹ Hawthorne.

Concord, Dec. 8th, 1860.

Dear Ticknor,

I find that my cash balance at the bank is getting very low; and as I have some immediate payments to make on account of the new house, I wish you would give me another credit for $500.

I find the weather terribly cold this morning — colder than I have known it for eight years.

Your friend,

Nathl Hawthorne.

Concord, Decr 9th, 1860.

Dear Ticknor,

The study table is all right; and I am writing this note at it in my new study.

Business is now so dull that I should think you might find time to come and smoke a cigar with me in this comfortable room. The rest of the tower is not yet finished.

I told some marble manufacturers, whose names I have forgotten, to send you their bill for fireplaces — sixty dollars or thereabouts.

Is there going to be a general smash?

Your friend,

Nathl Hawthorne.

Concord, Decr 28th, 1860.

Dear Ticknor,

My building expenses will amount to about $550 dollars more than I have hitherto paid;

and I shall have to draw upon your inexhaust-
ible resources to that amount. This will make
the cost of my additions somewhat more than
$2000;—the original estimate having been
only $500. Well, I suppose I am fortunate
in getting off so cheap; but if I had known
how much it was to cost me, I think I should
have sold the old house and bought a better
one.

I shall want some money soon for other
expenses; so you may as well send me a check
for $600, or $700, if convenient.

Are times so terribly bad as people say? I
have left off reading newspapers, and only
know by hearsay that the Union is falling
asunder.

I want to see you very much, but cannot
conveniently leave home at this season;—the
first train starting so early, and the second so
late.

Your friend,

Nath¹ Hawthorne.

Concord, Jany 30th, '61.

Dear Ticknor,

Here is a bill sent me by poor Driscoll's administrators, in which I find an error of $8. I bespoke two pair of their check pantaloons; but by some mistake, only one pair was sent, and I afterwards countermanded the other pair. Mr. Devereux will remember the circumstance.

Please not to forget that I have a payment to make on or before the fifth (5th) of the coming month, and should like a cheque for 300 or 400 dollars, in season for it. If I escape absolute beggary, I shall thank Heaven and you. What will be the use of having a house, if it costs me all my means of living in it?

Mrs. Hawthorne was completely delighted with the beautiful set of Waverley novels; and I myself took very great pleasure in arranging them on the shelf. As soon as I have money to spare, I am going to spend it in filling up some bookcases.

Your friend,

Nathl Hawthorne.

Concord, Feby 15th, 1861.

Dear Ticknor,

I suppose the enclosed bill, or one similar to it, will be sent to you; and you will much oblige me by paying it.

You have not yet been to see us; and I have hardly the heart to ask you, till our place shall look a little less dreary. The melting of the snow discloses so much rubbish to be removed, in the vicinity of the house, that I fear we shall not have a decent lawn for several months to come. Within doors, we are getting arranged by slow degrees.

I spend two or three hours a day in my sky-parlor, and duly spread a quire of paper on my desk; but no very important result has followed, thus far. Perhaps, however, I shall have a new Romance ready, by the time New England becomes a separate nation — a consummation I rather hope for than otherwise.

Your friend,

Nath¹ Hawthorne.

Concord, May 16th, 1861.
Dear Ticknor,

I shall want some more money (say $100) in the course of a day or two.

I should also like some Marsala wine, by way of cheap and wholesome drinking. It is good enough for me, and for people in general; but whenever you come to see me, you shall taste the best liquor I have.

The war continues to interrupt my literary industry; and I am afraid it will be long before Romances are in request again, even if I could write one. I wish I could turn my hand to any useful labor. If I were younger, I would volunteer; but as the case stands, I shall keep quiet till the enemy gets within a mile of my own house.

The house, by the by, is finished and painted, and really makes a very pretty appearance. It is odd, however, that I have never felt so earnest a desire to go back to England as now that I have irrevocably planted myself at home.

Your friend,

Nath¹ Hawthorne.

Concord, May 26th, '61.

Dear Ticknor,

Bridge has sent me $545*—being $500 principal and $45 interest on his note; so please to endorse this amount on the note. It comes unexpectedly, but not inopportunely; for I have a payment of about that amount to make soon.

Burchmore writes me that he has got a place as watchman at the Navy Yard which will keep him from starving. He would like to have his watch again, and I shall either send or bring it to you shortly. He must have it without refunding the $20; for he can be in no condition, at present, to pay debts.

I think my health is rather better than it has been for some time past; but I doubt whether I shall ever again be so well as I used to be in England. If I had established myself by the seashore instead of in this inland town, perhaps it would have been better; but I have fastened myself down by taking a house upon my back. It is folly for a mortal man to do anything more than pitch a tent.

*Five hundred forty-five Dollars.

I wish they would push on the war a little more briskly. The excitement had an invigorating effect on me for a time, but it begins to lose its influence. But it is rather unreasonable to wish my countrymen to kill one another for the sake of refreshing my palled spirits; so I shall pray for peace.

Your friend,

Nathl Hawthorne.

Concord, Octr 7th, 1861.

Dear Ticknor,

Bridge has unexpectedly sent me five hundred dollars, ($500.) which please to endorse on his note. This being the case, I shall not need the $100, for which I asked you through Fields; so please to reserve it for the next occasion.

You have not yet been to see us.

Your friend,

Nathl Hawthorne.

Concord, March 3d, 1862.

Dear Ticknor,

The magazines make a splendid addition to my book-shelves. I sincerely thank you for them.

I suppose Thursday holds good for our time of starting. I have forgotton at what hour we are to leave Boston, and will thank you to let me know.

Truly yours,

Nath[l] Hawthorne.

Concord, April 20th, '62.

Dear Ticknor,

I am happy to hear from Julian that you have returned from your wanderings and are safely established at the Old Corner again. If the trip has done you as much good as it did me, it is well worth the time and money.

Bridge paid me three hundred (300) dollars on his note, and will pay the balance when you inform him what the amount is.

I brought home some of your standing photographs (of which see a specimen,) as it was taken at the photographist's request, and there was nothing to pay. I hold them at your disposal.

I wish you would write to Derby about my large photograph. You know he promised me (and you too, for that matter) on behalf of Mr. Garden, that I should have a copy — which was my sole inducement for standing, because I know that Mrs. Hawthorne would like to have it. But, on speaking to Garden about it, the day before I left Washington, it appeared to me that he did not intend to give the copy.

Do come and see me. I want to talk over our travels, and your subsequent adventures.

Sincerely yours,

Nath¹ Hawthorne.

P. S.. Did you find in New York that Bixby has closed his hotel?

Ellsworth, Aug. 8th, '62.

Dear Ticknor,

We have got thus far on our way, after many hardships.

I have determined not to go to Mount Desert for two or three weeks to come. My direction for the present will be,

"Care of Mr. Barney Hill,
"Gouldsborough, Maine."

Fields said he should soon have a proof-sheet for me. It may be sent as above.

In haste,

Your friend,

Nath¹ Hawthorne.

P. S. The mail comes to Goldsborough only three times a week.

Concord, October 27th, '62.

Dear Ticknor,

I want a hundred dollars before Saturday, having my taxes to pay then.

How have you been this long while? I
mean to come to Boston for a day, when I get
through with some writing which I have now
in hand.

> Your friend,
>
> Nath¹ Hawthorne.

Concord, Janry 6th, 1863.

Dear Ticknor,

I want (as usual) a hundred dollars; and I
enclose a tailor's bill of Devereux & Eager,
which, at your leisure, I should like to have
you pay. It grieves me to have to impose
trouble of this sort upon you; but it is the
penalty of your own kindness, and kind people
always will be bothered by idle and incom-
petent ones.

I don't know whether I shall ever see you
again; for I have now staid here so long that
I find myself rusted into my hole, and could
not get out even if I wished.

> Your friend,
>
> Nath¹ Hawthorne.

Concord, Feby 8th, '63.

Dear Ticknor,

I am very sorry for our friend North, but hope he will consider there is more honor and comfort in being turned out than in being kept in by such a miserable administration as this. We are going to have great changes in our institutions; and I trust that one result will be, to prevent upright and capable men from being sacrificed merely on account of honest political opinions.

I have done nothing about my claim as Surveyor, and if Mr. North can push it through, I shall be glad both on his account and my own. He may make his own terms of remuneration. If he needs any information or assistance as to papers or records in the Salem Custom House, Burchmore would no doubt be able to give it to him, or get it for him. He is still, I suppose, a clerk in the Charlestown Navy Yard.

As Mr. North has written to you, I return my answer through the same medium, and you may inclose my note to him if you think proper.

When the weather gets a little more genial,

I shall come and see you. What became of the visit from General Pierce and yourself, which you promised me?

> Your friend,
>
> Nath¹ Hawthorne.

Concord, Feb 22d, 1863.

Dear Ticknor,

I knew that nobody but yourself could have sent me that cider, and it tastes all the more deliciously for that knowledge. I never drank any that I liked so well, and my wife agrees with me in opinion. We sit down quietly together, when everybody is gone to bed, and make ourselves jolly with a bottle of it.

I will try to write a few lines for Miss Harris, but don't know what in the world to say.

> Your friend,
>
> Nath¹ Hawthorne.

Concord, April 30th, 63.

Dear Ticknor,

I thank you for that excellent lot of cigars, and expect to have as much enjoyment as a

man can reasonably hope for in this troublesome world, while smoking them after breakfast and dinner. Their fragrance would be
much improved if you would come and smoke
in company.

Your friend,

Nathl Hawthorne.

Concord, June 18th, '63.

Dear Ticknor,

I sent you a week ago to-day, a sealed package containing an article for the Magazine;
and not hearing of its arrival, I deem it possible it may have miscarried — which would be
a pity, as I have no other copy. For reasons
connected with the publication of my volume,
I wanted this article to appear in the Magazine
as soon as possible.

But I suppose you do not concern yourself
about the Magazine.

I should have come to see you last week, if

it had not been so rainy; and now it is so hot
that I think I shall put it off till the autumn.

Your friend,

Nath¹ Hawthorne.

P. S.   I hear nothing of Fields.   Whereabouts is he?

Concord, July 27th, '63.

Dear Ticknor,

I have been looking over my quarterly bills,
and find that it will take more than $250 to
pay them; so, if you please, I should like $300
(three hundred) which will leave me very little
in pocket.   I expect to outlive my means and
die in the alms-house.   Julian's college expenses
will count up tremendously.   I must try to get
my poor blunted pen at work again pretty
soon; especially as Fields threatens me that
nobody will buy the new book on account of
the dedication.

Your friend,

Nath¹ Hawthorne.

Concord, Jany 7th, 1864.

Dear Ticknor,

I have received from the Merchants Bank two printed circulars, one of which inquires whether I am willing to surrender five of my shares and receive the par value thereof, and whether I will authorize the Directors to convert the Bank into a National Bank &c. Personally, I have no objection to either of these proposals, but as I know nothing about their expediency, I wish to be guided by your advice.

I had the great and unexpected pleasure of seeing Fields an hour or two ago, and feel much refreshed by the interview.

All my bills have not yet been sent in, but I suppose I shall want as much as $150 pretty soon; and so I take this occasion to mention it, though there is no hurry about it.

I have felt considerably better of late, and begin to be conscious of an inclination to resume the pen.

This is a terribly cold winter.

Most truly yours,

Nath¹ Hawthorne.

Concord, March 18th, '64.

Dear Ticknor,

I have gained strength a little, and am otherwise as flourishing as can be expected of a man in my desperate condition,— still retaining rapturous remembrances of the beef-steak and oysters. I am fully resolved to start on Wednesday, or any day thereafter that may suit your conscience. I have heard from Pierce, who does not go with us. Let me know your final decision as to the day.

Your friend,

Nath¹ Hawthorne.

END OF VOLUME II.

INDEX

THE MARION PRESS
JAMAICA QUEENSBOROUGH NEW YORK